MOTIVATING STUDENTS IN INFORMATION LITERACY CLASSES

TRUDI E. JACOBSON AND LIJUAN XU

NEAL-SCHUMAN PUBLISHERS, INC.

NEW YORK   LONDON

The New Library Series

Published by Neal-Schuman Publishers, Inc.
100 William Street, Suite 2004
New York, NY 10038

Copyright © 2004 by Trudi E. Jacobson and Lijuan Xu
IBSN 1-55570-497-2

Printed and bound in the United States of America.

The paper used in this publication meets the minimum requirements of American National Standard for Informational Sciences — Permanence of Paper for Printed Library Materials, ANSI Z39.48 — 1992

Cataloging-in-Publication Data for this book is available from the Library of Congress, record number 2004046007.

areas in a very understandable manner, Keller's model is a very practical framework for thinking about various motivating techniques. We link most ideas back to this model as a useful structure. In this chapter we will differentiate between intrinsic and extrinsic motivation, and explain why we concentrate on one rather than the other.

Chapter 2, "The Use of Motivational Theories in Various Instructional Models," takes a look at ways to develop courses and classes using the frameworks suggested by research on motivation. While the emphasis of this book is on credit courses, this chapter considers other forms, such as course-related instruction, drop-in sessions, and training connected to first-year experience programs and learning communities.

Part II, "How to Build Motivation into Instruction," explores the fundamentals of using those elements important for motivating students. Beginning in this section, you will find handy instructor tips, sidebars that relate our actual experiences, and examples of exercises and assignments. You can use these proven examples as is, or as jumping-off points for your own ideas. One of the things we love most about teaching is the ability to be creative. In developing our courses in order to maximize student motivation, we have found fertile ground for originality and new ideas. We hope that some of what we have written will in turn spark your imagination. Be assured that many of the ideas are easily adaptable to your own situation.

Chapter 3, "Initial Course Design" will help enhance student motivation, even before class begins. We describe and illustrate ways to design a course, the teaching methods that you may adopt, and the assignments that you might want to develop, in order to achieve this goal. It also includes methods of instruction, course assignments, course syllabus, and the first day of class.

Chapter 4, "Better Teaching Behaviors," explores enthusiasm, clarity, and interaction. Teaching behaviors can enhance, or quickly squash, student motivation. We briefly review elementary ones. Others are less evident, and we explain in more depth.

Chapter 5, "Active Learning Techniques," explores active learning in the classroom, cooperative learning, writing to learn, discovery learning, and key characteristics of active learning techniques.

Chapter 6, "Student Autonomy," looks at student choices, some caveats, and ways to encourage autonomy. A number of methods provide students with decision-making power, which is shown to increase motivation, without turning over the reins of the entire class to them. We describe some of the best methods.

Chapter 7, "Authentic Assessment," surveys the definitions of authentic assessment—the emphasis on application and use of knowledge rather than measuring isolated skills. Instructors have the power of assessment and grading in our courses, and can use authentic assessment tools as a powerful motivator. We explore a number of tools, with examples.

Chapter 8, "Online Teaching Situations," covers online instruction and techniques for increasing motivation in online classes. Some instructors teach Web-based classes, while others use some components of online instruction in otherwise more traditional classes. We investigate various permutations of online teaching and motivational techniques for these settings.

We hope that the ideas we suggest will serve as a springboard for you. Feel free to use any of the exercises or activities in the following chapters. Some may be useful without adaptation, but you will find ways to revise, enhance, and embellish others for your own unique situation. We hope you enjoy the process of motivating your students, as much as we do. The change in classroom climate and the increase in student engagement and learning make the effort extremely worthwhile.

References

Keller, John M. 1987a. Strategies for Stimulating the Motivation to Learn. *Performance & Instruction* 26, no. 8 (October): 1–7.

Keller, John M. 1987b. The Systematic Process of Motivational Design. *Performance & Instruction* 26, nos. 9/10 (November/December): 1–8.

Acknowledgments

We would like to thank our University Libraries (UNL) teaching team colleagues, past and present, for all the enthusiasm, ideas, and support you have provided during this exciting adventure. We would also like to thank our UNL 205 students, and our students in other settings, who have made teaching such a joy, and who, by their responses, have taught us a great deal about the art of teaching.

To Carol Anne Germain, Ellen Keith, and Thomas Mackey, we owe a debt of gratitude for reading the manuscript and for providing such wonderful suggestions. We appreciate all the conversations we have had with each of you about teaching; you are fabulous sources of inspiration and energy.

Our sincerest thanks to the librarians and professors who shared assessment techniques, exercises, case studies and other wonderful ideas that we have included in this volume:

Carol Anderson, University at Albany
Susan E. Beck, New Mexico State University
Deborah Bernnard, University at Albany
Carol Anne Germain, University at Albany
Stephan J. Macaluso, State University of New York at New Paltz
Thomas P. Mackey, School of Information Science and Policy,
    University at Albany
Robert Mumper, State University of New York at New Paltz

We also incorporated ideas from a number of others, as described in published sources; and these are cited throughout the chapters.

As always, Trudi would like to thank John, for his never-ending encouragement and his wonderful advice.

Part I:
Motivational Theory for Instruction

Chapter 1
Motivation and Learning Theory

When talking about student motivation, two classroom scenarios come to mind. In the first one, students are attentive and active. They respond to questions and react to the comments the instructor makes. It takes little effort on the instructor's part to promote discussions. In the second scenario, students sit passively, their faces unresponsive. Some of the students are busy doing "important" work for other courses, while others are chatting, dozing off, or playing on the computer. The instructor has to exert a lot of effort to get them to pay attention. Sometimes it seems that no matter how hard and whatever the instructor tries, students remain passive, and as soon as the class is over, they rush eagerly out of the classroom. For those of us who are teaching, the first class scenario is enjoyable, as well as satisfying to teach, and we look forward to the next class meeting. The second class-scenario is what we would like to avoid. Every time we teach such a class, we probably feel as if we are fighting a losing battle, and we dread the next class meeting. Fortunately, most classes do not go to the extreme of the second scenario; rather, they often contain some students who are motivated and some who are less motivated. Why do students differ in the level of motivation and effort they show in class? What motivates them to learn? How can we teach in a way that will enhance their motivation and learning?

John Keller, a specialist in instructional systems and educational psychology, thinks that "[i]t is possible to create conditions that will stimulate people's desire to be interested and involved in their surroundings and to achieve their best" (Keller, 1987b: 1). He goes on to suggest that before the instructors can decide on what motivational techniques to use, they first need to have a basic understanding of motivation: its primary components and strategies that have positive

3

influence on these components (Keller, 1987b: 1). Teachers can select from various motivation theories and models. In this book, we focus on two of them: intrinsic vs. extrinsic motivation and Keller's ARCS (Attention/Relevance/Confidence/Satisfaction) Model.

Learning Theories

Learning and motivation are two closely related concepts. In our research into motivation, we considered learning theories and the connection between learning and motivation. Understanding how students learn will help us better understand how to motivate them to learn at their best. Out of the vast research done in this area, we only discuss a limited number of learning theories briefly.

Three main schools of learning shape modern approaches to education: behaviorism, cognitive psychology, and humanist psychology. While behaviorism emphasizes the use of reinforcement, cognitive psychology focuses on relating the new material to what learners already know. The humanist theory overlaps a great deal with cognitive psychology; however, in addition, it considers the learners' feelings. "No one single theory or theorist can be singled out as having the complete, right answer about how people learn" (Grassian and Kaplowitz, 2001: 55). Each has its own application for teaching and learning.

Intrinsic versus Extrinsic Motivation

Motivation is "the process of initiating, sustaining, and directing activity" (McGregor, 1999: 39). When students are motivated, they have more interest and desire to learn. Motivation can derive from either intrinsic or extrinsic forces. The extrinsic motivators come from external forces and are often materialized. The intrinsic forces come from within, "usually in the form of intangible personal satisfactions, such as feelings of self-determination and competence" (Lowman, 1990: 137).

Extrinsic Motivation

Educators divide extrinsic motivators into two categories: positive reinforcement, such as candy, extra points, and certificates; and negative reinforcement, such as point or grade deduction. When educators motivate students extrinsically, they drive students to learn, because of their desire to obtain rewards or to avoid punishment. Joseph Lowman, a

Behaviorism	• Deals with observable behavior • Immediate feedback must follow desired behavior for it to be learned/continued while undesired behavior should never be reinforced. • Active participation is crucial. • Learners should be allowed to learn at their own pace, and they should be tested for mastery at each stage.
Cognitive Psychology	• Deals with the organization of information. • Interested in how various elements, ideas, and topics relate to one another. • Insight and the motivation to reduce ambiguity are viewed as underlying learning. • Mismatches between new experiences and the learner's current mental models lead to more complex modes of thinking.
Humanist Psychology	• Feelings and concerns are as important as thinking and behaving. • Learners determine their own behavior, and are free to make choices. • Material must have personal meaning or relevance. • Learners are felt to be intrinsically motivated.

Figure 1–1 Characteristics of Learning Theories (Grassian and Kaplowitz, 2001: 36–52)

psychology professor, argues that "students can be motivated to learn anything if promised a sufficiently attractive external reward" (1990: 137). For some students, their fear of punishment can also serve as the inducement for them to learn. For example, if a student needs the credit to graduate and he or she is afraid of failing the course, then the student will put more effort and time into the course, just to avoid the possible result—failing the course and therefore not being able to graduate.

Although extrinsic motivators are very powerful and can quickly get students to master new behaviors and modify their existing behaviors, the educator must offer rewards indefinitely for the desired behavior to continue. For example, if you reward students with extra points for their participation in class, they will expect to receive the same incentive again next time, and if they receive no reward, they will most likely sit back and relax in class. The same rule applies to the use of the negative reinforcement method. If you penalize students for not attending class, or for late arrival, you need to apply the penalty on a continuous and consistent basis for it to be effective.

However, Forsyth and McMillan recommend minimizing the use of either type of extrinsic motivators (55). Positive and negative reinforcement can both lower a student's sense of self-determination and control; and extrinsic motivators can actually discourage students from learning what you want them to learn, if students perceive thereby your controlling role as the only authority in the classroom. And when students are rewarded for doing something that already intrinsically appeals to them, it can shift their reason for undertaking the activity from inherent interest in the activity itself, to external rewards, which in turn decreases students' satisfaction in performing the task (Raffini, 1993: 75). In addition, when we motivate students extrinsically, they "perform the task because of the value or importance they attach to what the outcome brings" (Biggs, 1999: 59). Their minds and energy tend to focus on the type of the material consequence elicited by their learning—reward or punishment—instead of what lies in the learning process and the intrinsic worth of the activities themselves. Therefore, the quality of their learning is usually low (Biggs, 2000: 59).

Intrinsic Motivation

In contrast to extrinsic motivation, "intrinsic motivation is innate to the human organism and is part of an ongoing pattern in which people are driven to seek out and to master challenges that match their capabilities" (Raffini, 1993: 65). Intrinsic motivators are purer and pertain more to the subject matter itself (Nilson, 1998: 57). When educators motivate students intrinsically, they learn because they are fascinated by the subject/task, and they gain pleasure out of learning the subject and/or performing the task. This kind of interest- and satisfaction-driven student needs little to no guidance or supervision from the instructor. They pay keen attention to the class, they participate actively in various learning activities, and their effort goes beyond what we ask them to do in class.

Compared to extrinsic motivators, intrinsic motivators take effect more slowly, but "are usually more lasting once they take hold" (Lowman, 1990: 137). Intrinsic motivation also "drives deep learning and the best academic work" (Biggs, 1999: 60). Under intrinsic motivation conditions, students have their minds set on the activity itself and on what takes place during the learning process, rather than the material consequences of their learning.

To increase students' intrinsic motivation, the instruction and learning activities need to challenge students, stimulate their interest, and give them a sense of control over their own success (Raffini, 1993: 69–71). They should have the appropriate level of difficulty so that they will not only match, but also challenge, the various skill levels of the students. This way, each student will feel challenged and will also have a chance to succeed; the activities should reflect students' background and experiences, and appeal to students' sense of curiosity. Exercises should promote students' feelings of self-determination and autonomy by allowing students some choice over what to do. Cooperative learning activities and other activities that give students opportunities to apply what they have learned are two examples (Lowman, 1990: 137–138).

ARCS Model

John Keller developed the ARCS (Attention, Relevance, Confidence, Satisfaction) Model, "based on a general theory of motivation in relation to learning, and on supporting studies from many areas of research on human motivation" (Keller, 1987a: 2). The model suggests four prerequisites for student motivation, and it also recommends strategies in meeting each of these four conditions.

Major Categories & Definitions		Major Process Questions
Attention	Capturing the interest of learners; stimulating the curiosity to learn	*"How is learning valuable and stimulating to my students?"*
Relevance	Meeting the personal needs/goals of the learner to effect a positive attitude	
Confidence	Helping the learners to believe/feel that they will succeed and control their success	*"How can I (via instruction) help students succeed and allow them to control their outcomes?"*
Satisfaction	Reinforcing accomplishment with rewards (internal and external)	

Figure 1–2 Components of Keller's ARCS Model (Keller, 1987a: 2)

Attention

To motivate students to learn, the instructor must first get students to pay attention to what is presented and then keep them interested in the subject and/or activity. "In the learning process, a student's attention has to be directed to the appropriate cues, but before it can be directed, it has to be acquired" (Keller, 1987a: 1). New teaching approaches, injecting instructors' personal experiences in the class, posing questions, and any sudden change in the environment, including voice level, will serve to capture students' attention and stimulate their curiosity in the material. Varied activities and presentation styles will also keep students from getting bored.

Relevance

In order to maintain student interest in the material or subject matter, they will have to perceive that it is related to their personal goals. Nobody wants to learn something that seems to be worthless to him or her; therefore, the material must be personally relevant to students. To generate relevance, educators should tie their instruction to students' own experiences, and illustrate the connections between the content and the matters that students prioritize. The use of various strategies, such as individual activities, cooperative activities, and leadership roles, will help match the class with the different levels and learning styles of the students and increase relevance.

Confidence

After establishing the relevance of the instruction, you need to build an appropriate level of student confidence. To instill confidence in students is to help them "believe/feel that they will succeed and control their success" (Keller, 1987a: 2). One of the simplest ways to build student confidence is to let them know what you expect of them. That requires you to design instruction and related learning activities to match the different skill levels of the students. They should be neither too easy, nor too difficult; so that each student will have a chance to succeed after some effort. "The successful experience will be meaningful and will stimulate continued motivation if there is enough challenge to require a degree of effort to succeed, but not so much that it creates serious anxieties or threatens failure" (Keller, 1987a: 4).

Satisfaction

The last motivational requirement that you need to meet is satisfaction. For students "to have a continuing desire to learn, [they] must have a sense of satisfaction with the process or results of the learning experience" (Keller, 1987a: 2). To promote satisfaction, the educator should design instruction to allow students to apply their newly acquired knowledge or skill. Such strategies can include case studies, simulations and experiential learning activities. Positively reinforcing students' success will also enhance their sense of satisfaction. When your class meets all four of the conditions described above, students will be continuously motivated to learn.

Keller's ARCS Model falls under humanist psychology (Grassian and Kaplowitz, 2001: 53), but it ties closely to the other theories, particularly the cognitive theory. It is simple and easy to understand. The progressive approach—first getting and keeping attention, then creating relevance, and then building confidence and satisfaction—presents an explicit way of thinking about and implementing various motivating techniques. When a technique is not working, you can measure it against the model to find out what element is missing and how you can improve it. The ARCS Model provides a practical framework for teaching and motivating students to learn.

In this book, we focus on intrinsic motivation and Keller's ARCS Model, and we discuss how to motivate students through initial course design, teaching behaviors, active engagement of students, student autonomy, and authentic assessment.

References

Biggs, John. 1999. *Teaching for Quality Learning at University*. Buckingham, England: Society for Research into Higher Education and Open University Press.

Forsyth, Donelson R., and James H. McMillan. 1991. Practical Proposals for Motivating Students. In *College Teaching: From Theory to Practice*, edited by Robert J. Menges and Marilla D. Svinicki. New Directions for Teaching and Learning, no. 45 (Spring): 53–65.

Grassian, Esther S., and Joan R. Kaplowitz. 2001. *Information Literacy Instruction: Theory and Practice*. New York: Neal-Schuman.

Keller, John M. 1987a. Strategies for Stimulating the Motivation to Learn. *Performance & Instruction* 26, no. 8 (October): 1–7.

———. 1987b. The Systematic Process of Motivational Design. *Performance & Instruction* 26, nos. 9/10 (November/December): 1–8.

Lowman, Joseph. 1990. Promoting Motivation and Learning. *College Teaching* 38, no. 4 (Fall): 137–139.

McGregor, Joy H. 1999. How Do We Learn? In *Learning and Libraries in an Information Age: Principles and Practice,* edited by Barbara K. Stripling, 25–53. Englewood, CO: Libraries Unlimited.

Nilson, Linda B. 1998. *Teaching at Its Best: A Research-Based Resource for College Instructors.* Bolton, MA: Anker Publishing.

Raffini, James P. 1993. *Winners Without Losers: Structures and Strategies for Increasing Student Motivation to Learn.* Boston: Allyn and Bacon.

Chapter 2
The Use of Motivational Theories in Various Instructional Models

While the primary audience for this book is librarians who are teaching, or plan to teach, credit-bearing information literacy courses, a number of the theories and techniques described here apply to students in a much broader range of library instruction and information literacy models. Not every institution currently offers information literacy courses: institutions meet student information literacy needs in a variety of ways that work for their own settings. Some libraries may focus on course-related instruction, either in courses related to the major, or perhaps connected with a required English course. Others might concentrate on freshmen year experience programs or learning communities.

This chapter examines the following learning models:

- Course-related instruction
- Drop-in sessions
- First year experience programs/learning communities
- Credit-bearing courses

In each case, we will address motivating factors generally applicable to the setting, along with the model's limitations in regard to student motivation. Also, we will highlight specific options from later chapters that are most appropriate or feasible.

Course-Related Instruction

Librarians on many campuses provide instruction to students in a wide variety of courses. This instruction model generally involves one session with students in a course, but may be more involved than that. Librarians work closely with faculty members to design instruction sessions that meet the needs of the students for that particular course, but may also involve more general instruction that students will find useful during their academic careers.

Motivating Factors

One extremely important factor that affects motivation in course-related instruction is the existence of a research assignment. Librarians know that this factor is effective in getting and holding student attention. If the instruction session is timed well, students will be aware of the assignment. They will have given it some thought, but will not yet be panic-stricken. They will find the class relevant, Keller's second motivational requirement, if the material taught is directly related to this upcoming assignment.

A second important factor is the value that the faculty member places upon the instruction session. Librarians have all come across faculty members, who schedule a library class on a day when they will be out of town. The professor's attitude toward a library session can go a great way toward enhancing student motivation. Every librarian who has taught numerous sessions will remember instructors whose attitudes have focused student attention by impressing upon them the importance of the material. Conversely, librarians may also recall instructors whose behaviors (such as grading papers or searching the Web) during class have caused students to question the value of the session. Address this issue with each professor prior to instruction sessions. Sometimes they just do not realize that they are conveying a negative or even a neutral attitude, or that it has such an effect on student learning and motivation during library instruction sessions.

Librarians may not have a great deal of influence on assignments or faculty attitudes (other than to develop or enforce a policy requiring assignments and/or faculty presence). Librarians more directly control the design of the instruction session and their own behavior in the classroom, and these elements intersect with Keller's confidence and satisfaction concepts. You can build confidence through active learning methods. Satisfaction will generally come after the class, when students are working on the assignment, or have gotten positive feedback on it from their professor.

Limitations

Two factors that have a serious negative impact on course-related instruction are lack of time with the students, and little or no continuity. In most course-related instruction, librarians teach students once, for approximately 50 to 80 minutes. While this provides some time to implement motivating methods, that time is severely limited. In addition, it does not allow you to set the stage or follow up later, unless you have made special arrangements with the professor or with individual students. Some motivation techniques take time, or build upon earlier class sessions, and require that you meet with students a number of times. Others call for you to have control over a number of course design elements. These obviously will not apply to course-related sessions, unless you have the opportunity to work very closely with the professor who designs the course.

Working with Course Faculty to Enhance Motivational Opportunities

The ideal course-related instruction situation enables you to help develop or design course material and assignment(s) to enhance each student's information literacy skills. Some faculty members do welcome such consultation. This may come about with new faculty members, or with established faculty who are developing new courses, redesigning existing courses, or working with other faculty to design team-taught interdisciplinary courses. Unless the faculty member asks a librarian to help with course design, it may require a great deal of tact to offer your assistance. However, if you do have a role during the design stage, many more of the suggested motivational techniques will be available to you. You will have the opportunity to extend the reach of the information literacy elements, and you will also be able to build in elements to heighten motivation. Course-related instruction will have metamorphosed into course-integrated instruction. For these situations, take a close look at Chapter 3, on Initial Course Design, as will Chapter 6, Student Autonomy, and Chapter 7, Authentic Assessment.

Most Appropriate Motivational Options

Librarians who engage in traditional course-related instruction should particularly consider their behaviors in the classroom, and their methods for actively engaging students. You can easily incorporate elements highlighted in Chapter 4, Better Teaching Behaviors, into a single class: enthusiasm, clarity of instruction, and interaction all can affect student motivation. In addition, even in one short session, it is quite possible to include active learning and/or discovery learning activities, and to use writing to learn techniques (see Chapter 5, Active Learning Techniques). These factors will positively influence student attention and student confidence. You can make direct ties to the course assignment, or to other issues of interest to students, to boost relevance of the class material. While some motivational techniques discussed in this book do not apply to this situation, quite a few do.

Drop-In Sessions

A number of academic libraries offer classes that are open to anyone affiliated with the institution. These classes might teach the latest programs and technologies connected to developing Web pages, the key sources in a specific discipline, or how to search for research materials most effectively. These sessions have some similarities to course-related sessions, but also some differences, as explained below.

Motivating Factors

The critical motivation factor is that students elect to attend these sessions. In most cases, they are not required to attend (unless there is a program requirement). Their own interest in library research intrinsically motivates students to learn the content. We can take methods for capturing attention and showing relevance as givens to some degree. In addition, the design of the class should highlight confidence and satisfaction. The Sagamore Design Model provides techniques that are appropriate for building confidence and satisfaction, particularly in technology-based drop-in sessions (Masie and Wolman, 1989: 76–83). This model incorporates both guided and unguided practice. After each section of new material, students engage in guided practice sessions to build their confidence, and unguided practice aimed at building satisfaction, which "allows learners to apply their newly learned skills and procedures to actual work or at least to realistic...tasks" (Masie and Wolman, 1989: 81).

Limitations

The limitations for drop-in sessions mirror those of course-related sessions, without the potential opportunity to work closely with a faculty member. Depending on your target audience, you might be able to develop a linked series of classes or workshops; however, unless attendees are highly motivated, they may not attend numerous workshops. In most cases, instructors of drop-in sessions will have the scope of one session for using motivational techniques.

Most Appropriate Motivational Options

Using motivational teaching behaviors is always appropriate, and will help to maintain the intrinsic motivation level that students brought with them to the session. Because these sessions often draw a disparate group of attendees, it is important to determine their goals for the class, and to design the session to meets their needs. Situations where the instructor must do this on the spot require quick thinking and a good deal of flexibility. If you are prepared to teach various levels and aspects of the subject matter, you can select the most relevant material that best meets the requirements of the students who attend.

Active learning exercises (see Chapter 5, Active Learning Techniques) are well suited to most drop-in sessions. For hands-on classes, they are critical, particularly for building student confidence and satisfaction, and for enhancing student learning. Other motivational techniques will depend upon student goals and course material.

First Year Experience Programs/Learning Communities

Numerous colleges and universities have developed learning models targeted toward freshmen. Each school structures its individual freshman-year experience, or learning communities, differently, with varying roles for librarians and for research-related instruction. In some cases, librarians share teaching responsibilities with other instructors, to teach students key information literacy skills. Some programs may build in extensive information management modules, taught entirely or in part by program faculty. Librarians might team-teach with program faculty, or they might be responsible for discrete segments. Because of program variations, the following sections contain somewhat equivocal suggestions that will depend upon your particular situation.

Motivating Factors

Students in freshman year experience programs or learning communities interact closely. Together, they take a number of linked courses, and in many cases live in the same dorm. This close-knit relationship frequently serves as a strong motivating factor. Students connected to one another in this way will be more involved in projects, and often more motivated when learning about ways to do research for these projects. This community context heightens both the attention and relevance factors. If the librarian is a key team member, students will view him or her differently than if the librarian is seen just as a guest lecturer. Application of new skills will instill confidence, and students will experience increased satisfaction, because frequently colleges structure these programs to increase the connections between course content and the ever-growing base of knowledge and skills being mastered by students.

Limitations

Such programs will vary a great deal in design, and limitations will vary accordingly. Librarians are key players in some programs, while they are less directly involved in others. The amount of contact they have with students will vary, as will their input into assignments using newly honed research skills. Unless a librarian is integral to the program, a number of the same limitations found in course-related instruction will apply. If a librarian is a vital program participant, and if the program is large, he or she may find that it just is not possible to be as involved as the program might permit.

Most Appropriate Motivational Options

As with the limitations, motivational options will vary depending on the program design. If a librarian is very closely involved with the development of course assignments and course structure, many of the ideas presented in the following chapters will be appropriate. Also, because programs change over time, it might be possible to suggest more involvement, leading to increased opportunities for motivation and learning.

Credit-Bearing Courses

Credit-bearing information literacy courses provide students with the opportunity to gain a deeper knowledge of information-related concepts and skills. They provide a host of opportunities for encouraging student motivation; however, different types of information literacy courses have their own characteristics. This section will examine these characteristics, and their influence upon student motivation.

Discipline-Specific versus Generic Courses

Institutions relate some information literacy courses to a particular discipline or field of study. An example would be a new course, East Asian Research and Bibliographic Methods, at the University at Albany, of the State University of New York (also called SUNY Albany). This course includes important, basic information literacy concepts; however, the professor teaches them against the background of, and uses examples and assignments drawn directly from, the field. Generic information literacy courses do not have this disciplinary focus. They may contain students in a range of majors, and instructors must design the material to meet the needs of everyone in the class.

Motivating Factors and Limitations

If a school ties an information literacy course to a particular major, students will more obviously see the relevance to their lives. Skills learned in generic information literacy courses may easily transfer to a host of other assignments, courses, and subjects, but students do not always, or easily, make the link. When you directly relate the material to other courses that students are taking, they immediately perceive the connection. In addition, faculty members from a given department, rather than librarians, may teach information literacy courses specific to their discipline. Both students and librarians will undoubtedly recognize these professors as authorities in their fields of study, fields students inherently understand. Based on a professor's stature, she or he can more quickly gain the confidence of students, and can more immediately gratify their satisfaction. For pragmatic students, skills learned in the information literacy course will be closely tied to assignments for this and other courses in the discipline, and the anticipation of using new knowledge immediately will positively affect student motivation.

Generic information literacy courses do not initially excite students' attention in the same way as discipline-specific courses, and the relevance of what they are learning is often not as immediately apparent. Instructors of such courses must plan carefully to build into the course as much relevance as possible. Rather than assign project topics to students, encourage students to select a topic that grows out of another course. When you can directly link an information literacy course project to another course's assignment, relevancy skyrockets. To improve the level of attention in class, it is critical not only to reinforce the idea that students can take what they are learning in a generic information literacy course into their other courses, but also to prove how this works. Attention and relevance are the two key ARCS Model factors that you must plan for exceedingly carefully in generic information literacy courses.

Students might view information literacy courses taught by librarians with some perplexity. Regardless of the librarian's status on campus, some students just do not view librarians as faculty members, masters of a particular body of knowledge. The information you present to the class on the first day about your background and expertise can go a long way to dispel students' attitudes, and to increase attention. This information might include your credentials, research interests, publications, involvement in information literacy or pedagogical ventures on campus, and national professional service related to information literacy or other aspects of librarianship.

One-Credit versus Three-Credit Courses

Not all information literacy courses earn a full credit load. A number of information literacy courses earn one, or perhaps two, credits. These variations in credit load impact not only how much an instructor can teach and what you can expect students to learn during the course, but also how students view the course. This factor directly affects motivation.

Motivating Factors and Limitations

Students view three-credit courses more seriously. These courses fit the standard course mold, and are considered "real classes." Generally, students think of one-credit courses as easy and not worth a great deal of effort. Some students are surprised to find that one-credit information literacy courses have required readings, homework assignments, and projects, just like two- and three-credit courses. The brevity of single-credit courses, which may only meet for half a semester, may reinforce student bias against taking these courses seriously. Moreover, pass/fail grading only serves to magnify the situation. One-credit courses, whether they meet just one hour a week for a full semester, or two hours a week for half a semester, do not allow the librarian the same amount of contact time with students that they would have in a course carrying more credits. Intrinsic motivation takes time to build. While instructors have a number of techniques at their disposal to increase student motivation even in a one-credit course, these courses lack the temporal advantage held by full credit courses. They do, however, provide more time to implement motivational techniques than the three other methods of information literacy instruction examined earlier in this chapter.

To some students, brevity may be a blessing. If a campus requires an information literacy course, students might want it to be as short as possible. While librarians would have plenty to teach and do if we had a full three-credit course, students might prefer meeting their course obligation more quickly. Students might also be more willing to add a one-credit course to their full course load, whereas this might not be possible with a three-credit course.

Most Appropriate Motivational Options for Credit-Bearing Courses

All of the options in the following chapters (Part II) — initial course design, teaching behaviors, active learning techniques, student autonomy, and authentic assessment — apply to credit-bearing courses. You will find some fit your circumstances and teaching style better than others, but you have a wide array of motivational techniques at hand. Each chapter in Part II explains the motivational aspects of the topic, and provides a variety of examples to stimulate the development of ideas that will work in your classroom.

References

Masie, Elliott, and Rebekah Wolman. 1989. *The Computer Training Handbook.* Edition 3.1. Raquette Lake, NY: Tools for Training.

Part II
How to Build Motivation into Instruction

Chapter 3
Initial Course Design

Before instructors ever meet their students for the first time, they spend a great deal of effort developing the course syllabus. They think about assignments, decide how to set the stage for the course in the first class session, and thoroughly prepare, so that they will be ready when they walk into class at the start of the term. As instructors work on each of these elements, they need to consider student motivation; it is never too early. In fact, if you do not plan to motivate students at this stage of preparation, it will be hard to incorporate a number of crucial elements later on. Course design and design for motivation go hand-in-hand. This chapter considers the following six categories relating to initial course design.

- Course topics
- Course goals and objectives
- Methods of instruction
- Course assignments
- Course syllabus
- The first day of class

Course Topics

The classes that most academic librarians teach are filled with a wide spectrum of students. Their interests, abilities, backgrounds, and goals all vary widely. The reasons students enroll in our courses range from a sincere interest in the topic, to recognition that this course will help in their future studies or career, to filling an open time slot in their schedule, to a need for the credits, to a general education or department requirement. Students who are truly interested in the course material, as

23

well as students who strive to get As in all their courses, will react differently to the course than those in the latter categories. Lowman (1995: 195) suggests that instructors choose their initial class topics based on engagement of all students, thus, saving less obviously engaging topics for later in the course. It is easier to retain student interest after you successfully engage them in course material, than it is to recapture their interest once the course is underway, especially if they have already written it off. This of course meshes with Keller's category of attention: "capturing the interest of learners; stimulating the curiosity to learn" (1987: 2).

You will need to choose the optimal sequence for topics in an information literacy course. It is hard to teach students how to do effective searches, if you do not introduce Boolean operators until a few weeks into the course. However, instructors may sequence some portions of their courses based on how they learned, or on the chronology of the development of particular resources, or simply on personal bias. Making some changes in your course sequence might improve your ability to catch and retain the attention of students.

Figure 3-1: Instructor Tip: Topic Sequencing of Databases vs. Web Search Engines

It might seem more logical to teach the effective searching of online bibliographic databases before teaching students how to search Web search engines. Librarians think of databases as more authoritative, and wish students would use them more often than they do. However, students have more experience with Web search engines, and may find learning search tips and techniques for these tools more relevant to their daily lives. Would it be possible to switch the order and yet still teach students what they need to know about both types of resources in a logical way? Might this actually aid your cause? After having first endeavored to obtain appropriate search engine results and next evaluating them, students might then particularly appreciate how much work database search results might save them.

Course Goals and Objectives

Relax, this section is not about how to write goals and objectives. Rather, it will focus on the need to include a range of goals and objectives when you write them. Lowman advises that instructors include a range of challenges in your course, something you can do through the goals and objectives that you develop (1995: 198–199). If you include a variety of different types of goals, of differing levels of difficulty, you will be able to engage more students than if your goals are less diverse.

> ...The best college teachers design their classes actually to offer students a wide range of challenges. They expect students to master facts, demonstrate that they can think about what they have learned in a personally meaningful and intellectually complex way, and apply their learning to real-world examples. Also, they expect students to show an array of problem-solving skills, as well as a skeptical disposition, and be able to communicate their ideas effectively. Designing a course that has a wide range of goals ensures that students with different interests and abilities will find something that captivates and challenges them. More importantly, a wide range of objectives will stretch students intellectually and pique their imaginations, more than will an agenda that stresses only acquiring information. (Lowman, 1995: 198–199)

Information literacy courses have an edge in a number of these factors compared to courses in more theoretical disciplines. It is not difficult to include elements in information literacy courses that allow students to see connections to the real world, to develop problem-solving skills, and to learn to use skepticism when evaluating information sources. Instructors can build in mechanisms to help students learn to communicate what they are mastering in the course. What we have found, though, in student evaluations of our courses, is that it is harder for students to perceive that their intellects are being stretched in a generic information literacy course, than in subject-specific courses. It is important to consider this carefully when designing your course. (After you have taught the course once or twice, feedback from previous students can help improve future courses.) Do not be afraid of challenging students—we have always been amazed at how well they respond to tough challenges.

Teaching students about ideas can be a way to promote critical thinking and engagement in a course.

> If we want students to think about what we teach, then our teaching must focus on ideas. An idea, almost by definition, is something to think about. Ideas are the basic units of an academic discipline.... Ideas...are sufficiently general to be interesting and sufficiently narrow to be testable. To test them we must discuss evidence, and that is how interest in a course develops; that is how students can experience the excitement of scholarship and research. (Gray, 1993: 68–69)

Library professionals have long debated in teaching mechanics versus concepts. By its very nature, information literacy instruction weighs heavily on concepts. At the same time, acquiring very specific mechanics does not bode well for lifelong learners in this age of rapidly changing technology. You can take ideas beyond the concepts customarily taught by librarians, by relating them to situations in real life. Applying concepts that are relevant to student experiences can be extremely effective motivators in information literacy courses, because seeing the connection to something they already know moves them a step beyond the basics and helps them to expand their outlook.

The example in Figure 3–2 illustrates how designing situations in which students confront different ideas and opinions about censorship can be much more effective than simply telling them about some of the issues involved.

Exercise Example: Internet Filtering Policy

In this activity, ask small groups of students to play the role of city councilors, who need to decide on a policy for filtering (or not) the content accessible on Internet terminals at the public library in the town. Give the groups a list of conflicting issues raised by different constituencies about access to the Internet generally, and to specific Web sites in particular. Ask each group to develop a policy for the town's library. The ensuing discussions, focused around the idea of censorship, engage students very effectively as they attempt to come up with a solution to this case study.

Figure 3–2 Exercise Example: Internet Filtering Policy (King, 2001: 267–268.)

The challenge is to balance teaching immediately usable skills with teaching ideas alone. Instructors obviously do not want students to learn to be information literate just for the isolated pleasure of information literacy, but would like students to use their new knowledge. It is easy for instructors to develop skill objectives that enunciate just what it is we want students to be able to do (or do better) when they finish the course (Lowman, 1995: 200).

For a start, students in information literacy courses can use what they learn to help them in their other courses, so they need not delay the gratification of utilizing new skills and new knowledge. As students discover the immediate benefits of what they learn in information literacy courses, the relevance of the course material will become evident.

Instructors are able to design their courses so that they include a range of challenges, both relating to skills and to engaging ideas. The list in Figure 3–3 elucidates what we expect of students in our course. Both skills and ideas play a part.

In this example, it is evident how even a one-credit course can be designed to offer a variety of types of challenges and goals. A three-credit course will offer even more scope for doing so. It is important to caution instructors, in their enthusiasm to cover the bases, against establishing too many goals for the scope of one course. That simply overwhelms students, and as a result key goals will become lost in the profusion.

The more personally relevant you can make these challenges to the current and future needs of students, the more you will motivate them. Keller emphasizes the importance of building bridges between the course content and the "learner's needs, wants, and desires" (1987: 3). A goal orientation, where you relate student work toward future goals, such as having an easier time doing research in other courses or in graduate school, is an effective motivator.

Figure 3-3 Instructor Tip: Expectations of Students

In UNL 205, we expect students to

- master facts (e.g., what is the difference between a primary and secondary document), something we can check via the quizzes we give;
- apply their learning by finding the ten required types of sources in conjunction with a paper they are writing in another class;
- use their problem solving skills in numerous assignments. One of these assignments, to research a hot topic relating to information, asks them to think about a complex issue. They often are able to relate it to their own experiences;
- be skeptical, to evaluate, in the critical annotations they write each week; and
- communicate what they have learned, since this is what they do in their final presentation to the rest of the class.

Methods of Instruction

The methods of instruction that you plan to use in the course will dictate how you arrange your class time, what exercises or activities you will use, even what type of a room you need. If you plan to lecture, you may not need a hands-on classroom. A demonstration system may be all the technology necessary. If you would like students to work together in small groups, a room with chairs bolted to the floor will not be your first choice. Before you select your instructional methods, you must make the decision about incorporating methods that increase motivation. We discuss more about these methods in Chapter 5, "Active Learning Techniques." It is critical to plan for diverse teaching techniques very early in the process of developing or revising a course.

You will want to plan early to vary your teaching methods from class period to class period, and also within a given class. To make class engaging, you should decide on some of these techniques in the days just before you actually teach a period (it is important to be flexible); but, unless you think about these issues early, you may find some of your options limited. Each course topic will probably suggest to you one or two ways to teach the material. If you do not feel terribly creative about possible teaching methods for various topics, ask other librarians who teach the same material. Or even ask your students how they would find learning that topic most interesting or efficient.

Course Assignments

Assignments are tied to motivational issues in a number of ways. Discovery assignments, to be discussed in Chapter 5, often enhance student interest. Hands-on assignments that can be started in class can be designed to be effective motivators. Assignments that allow for student choice are ideally suited to motivating them. You need to consider all of these issues early, so that they will be reflected in the materials that you prepare.

Course Syllabus

Some students ask their instructors such basic questions, concerning things such as office hours and your e-mail address, that it makes instructors wonder if some students ever look at the course syllabus. Despite the concern that some students indeed do not read the syllabus, it is extremely important to have a descriptive one, which lays out many of the issues that are considered in this chapter. Students who feel that the course requirements are unclear, or that you have introduced additional responsibilities and requirements after the fact, can become unsettled or unhappy. A descriptive syllabus, with all course requirements and guidelines clearly outlined, should be available to students at the start of the course.

On the syllabus, make patently evident which aspects of the course you included to increase student motivation. You will be telling students about these features in class, but it is even better for students to see them reinforced in writing. If you will allow students topic choices, highlight this fact. If they will have choices in relation to grading, point it out. Include a section on the teaching methods you use and the reasons why you use them. If you require students to work in groups, explain why. The more information that you give students regarding the format and content of the course, the better. Syllabi that amount to no more than a listing of class meeting dates, topics of the day, and homework assignments do nothing to motivate students; nor do they serve as a mechanism for conveying to students the reasons why you do what you do.

A syllabus with all this information is longer than a barebones calendar for the course. Students may be surprised at the length of the document, but you can explain in the first class why you have included the information you have. Figure 3-4 provides a sample syllabus for one of our credit courses. It illustrates the inclusion of features relating to motivation, such as:

- Topic choice
- Assignment choice
- Teaching methods used
- Professional skills students will gain
- Extra credit options

> Printing the syllabus on some unusual color paper makes it easier for students to recognize and find it amongst all their other materials. Students have told us that, although they may be overloaded with paper from our course and others, the syllabus always stands out if it is printed in cherry pink, lilac, or some other distinctive color.

Sample Syllabus
Course: **UNL 205: Information Literacy**
Instructor: Professor Trudi Jacobson
Title: Coordinator of User Education Programs
Office Location: UL 107D
Phone: (518) 442–3581 Fax: (518) 442–3567
E-mail: tjacobson@uamail.albany.edu
Office Hours: Mondays, 2:00 to 3:00 p.m., or by appointment
Day and Time: Wednesday—9:05 a.m to 11:05 a.m., Section #6328

Figure 3–4: Sample Syllabus

Location: University Library Basement, Room LI-48
Course Web Page: http://library.albany.edu/usered/unl205

Description:

This is a one-credit, quarter course that fulfills the Information Literacy General Education requirement. It meets one day a week for seven weeks. Each class is two hours long.

The purpose of the course is to acquaint you with the processes of finding, organizing, using, producing, and distributing information in print, electronic, and other formats. You will learn about the flow of information in a variety of disciplines, how to be effective at the research process, how to access information in a variety of formats, and how to formulate effective searches on electronic databases and the Internet. You will be taught to evaluate the quality of Web-based and print information, and will become familiar with practical, social, and ethical issues relating to information.

Course Objectives and Competencies Expected:

Upon completion of this course, you should be able to:

1. Identify the effect that technology has had on information production and dissemination.
2. Describe a variety of information sources and tools you can use to access these information sources.
3. Develop an effective search strategy for finding information using access tools.
4. Identify and analyze the source, authority, and perspective of information sources.
5. Understand the difference between a research topic and a thesis statement. Be able to turn a topic into a thesis statement.
6. Apply knowledge of the APA (American Psychological Association) style by compiling a bibliography. Know how to write critical annotations.
7. Discuss current issues relating to information policy. Analyze the impact of these policies on information access for individuals and communities.

Professional Skills:

When you leave this class, you will have gained or honed the following skills that will be important in the workplace or in graduate school:

1. You will know where to look to find the information you need. If you don't know immediately, you will have strategies to determine where to look.
2. You will know that appropriate format, as well as creator and quality of the information, will affect where you look.
3. You will have effective skills for finding the information you need, without wasting time looking for it.
4. In conjunction with the knowledge you gain in your major, you will be an effective evaluator of the information you find. This will help you with your projects or reports.

Figure 3-4 continued

5. You will be a good resource for others whose information finding skills are weak.

These skills will increase your value to employers, as well as your skills when researching job opportunities and preparing for interviews.

Student Responsibilities:

Each student is expected to contribute to an environment conducive to the learning of all students. This contribution includes, but is not limited to:

- Respecting the opinion of others
- Being prepared to participate actively
- Taking responsibility for your learning and progress in the course
- Seeking help from the instructor as needed

Students are responsible for knowing and following the policies presented below. Students are also responsible for knowing and following the University policies outlined in the Undergraduate Bulletin (http://www.albany.edu/undergraduate_bulletin/regulations.html).

Instructional Methods:

This class will incorporate active learning techniques and will require a high level of student participation. Students will be responsible for taking part in class discussions. Some work will be done in small groups. I am a strong proponent of learning by doing and by discussing. There will not be a great deal of lecture during the course.

Class Policies:

1. It is always the responsibility of the student to know when assignments are due.
2. Class attendance policies are:
   - Because it is disruptive, students may not be allowed into class after the first 5 minutes
   - Students are responsible for all class work, so work done in class cannot be made up
   - If you have to leave class early, make arrangements for a time AFTER that class to pickup assignments; we do what we do in class when we do it, so attendance is important.
   - Once a quiz starts it is not possible to take it if you walk in late
   Please note: the weekly quizzes and participation parts of your grade add up to 35%.
3. Assignments are due on time. Late assignments will receive a grade of zero. Any difficulty related to timely submissions must be discussed BEFORE or as close to the due date as possible. Also, a printer problem or Web or ERes (the University's Electronic Reserve system) access problems are not acceptable reasons for late assignments. Electronic submissions are acceptable at the instructor's discretion.
4. All assignments must be typed unless otherwise noted. Any work longer than one page should be stapled in the upper left-hand

Figure 3-4 continued

corner. Do not hand in any assignment on spiral notebook paper.
5. Do not plagiarize. Plagiarism is not tolerated and will result in a failing grade.
6. *Failure to complete the Annotated Bibliography constitutes a failure for the entire course since it is equivalent to a final exam.*
7. Cell phone alarms must be turned off before class starts; the use of computers during class is restricted to instructional activities; food or drinks (other than water) are not allowed.

Scale

A   100—93
A-   92—90
B+   89—87
B   86—83
B-   82—80
C+   79—77
C   76—73
C-   72—70
D+   69—67
D   66—63
D-   62—60
E   59 and below

Grading and Course Requirements:

Grading (A-E grading system)
20%
Assignments: worksheets, writing exercises, and readings
10%
Weekly citation/annotation drafts
25%
Completed annotated bibliography
10%
Teaching session or final class presentation
20%
Participation in class (4 points per class)
15%
Quizzes

Research Project

Each week's assignment contributes to a cumulative project, an annotated bibliography on a topic that you select and that the instructor approves. The parts of the bibliography are due as follows:

Week Two: Your topic

Week Three: Books and reference books (4 citations, 2 annotations) and Preliminary Thesis Statement

Week Four: One scholarly and one popular Web site, annotate both.

Week Five: Three articles (1 scholarly print, 1 popular print, 1 full-text from an online database such as EBSCO, JSTOR or LexisNexis). Annotate all 3. Photocopy and submit the first page

Figure 3-4 continued

of each.

Week Six: One primary, one secondary source, and one additional resource (see below), all annotated.

Week Seven: Hand in the completed annotated bibliography.

The final annotated bibliography should contain ten items in alphabetical order:

- A book
- A reference source in book format
- A popular Internet Web site
- A scholarly Internet Web site
- A print article from a popular magazine or newspaper
- A print article from a scholarly journal
- A full-text article (from a source such as EBSCO, JSTOR or LexisNexis)
- One primary source
- One secondary source
- One additional resource from one of these categories: electronic reference source, government document, or multimedia source (this can be a video or audio clip mounted on the Web)

Your final annotated bibliography should be *in alphabetical order*. At the end of each annotation, put the type of source in parentheses, for example: (full-text article). Put your name at the top of the page, followed by *Annotated Bibliography*, then your thesis statement.

Use the APA brief style guide sheet passed out in class (also available at http://library.albany.edu/usered/style/main.html), the more complete listing from the University of Illinois (http://www.english.uiuc.edu/cws/wworkshop/index.htm, select "Bibliography Styles") or use the 5th edition of the *Publication Manual of the American Psychological Association* (Ref BF 76.7 P83 2001).

Teaching Session or Final Class Presentation

You may choose which of the following you would like to do. You are responsible for notifying me by the second week of class which option you have selected.

There is a document called "Public Speaking Anxiety" in the Jacobson UNL 205 folder on ERes, if you have concerns about speaking in front of the class. You might find it very helpful.

Teaching Session

If you opt for this, you will teach a topic to the rest of the class. You will have some choice in the topic, but the topics available will depend upon how many students select this option. It is important to discuss this with me, so that you will know your topic and teaching date as early as possible. Teaching sessions will run from 5–15 minutes, depending on the topic and your choice of teaching method. You will need to turn in a teaching session outline on the day you teach.

Final Class Presentation

If you choose this, you will make a 5 minute presentation on the last day of class. The presentation is to address the following:

Figure 3-4 continued

- The reason you selected your topic
- A brief summary of what you found
- Problems you ran into finding information
- Interesting or unusual information/sources you came across

Effective creativity in your presentation will be rewarded. This might include, but is not limited to, showing key Web sites or other visuals or using PowerPoint.

You will also need to hand in your presentation outline on the last day of class.

Reserve Readings:

Materials for this course will be available through E-Reserves (ERes), the University's Electronic Reserve system, which can be found at http://eres.ulib.albany.edu/ You will find suggested or required readings, links to Web sites, and links to key resources for the course on E-Reserves, so it is your responsibility to learn how to access it. You can get to materials for this course searching either by course number or course professor. The course professor is: infolit, not the name of your actual instructor. E-Reserves materials are password protected for this class. You will need Adobe Acrobat to view reserve articles. Adobe Acrobat is available on computers in the lecture center user rooms (LC 3 and 4) and in the user room in the University Library. If you need a copy of Adobe Acrobat for your own computer, it can be downloaded for free from the E-Reserves Web page.

A copy of the *Research Strategies* textbook is also available at the Reserve desk in the basement of the University Library.

Extra Credit: TILT Web-Based Modules (http://tilt1.ulib.albany.edu/):

If you complete all three modules of the TILT information literacy tutorial by class time on November 19 and e-mail your quiz results to me, I will give you extra credit: two points toward your final grade. (Note: the two point addition may raise your final course grade, if it is borderline). In order for me to know you have completed all three modules, you must register as a TILT user (using your SUNYCard barcode number), and go back in under this registration each time. You will have to e-mail your quiz results to me, or print them out and give them to me. Technical glitches occur with TILT, so do not leave this to the last minute if you plan to do it. All TILT quiz results must be in by class time on November 19. No other extra credit assignments are available.

Course Outline:

October 22/Class 1:

Introduction, students' introductions

Pre-test

Information Literacy Video

Review of syllabus and class policies

The impact of technologies on information and information seeking behavior

Figure 3-4 continued

Information literacy concepts
Virtual Tour of University Library
Assignment: **Due at the beginning OR BEFORE (Item #3)**
Class 2
1. Type one page (double-spaced) in which you define your own information-seeking behavior. Survey one other person on his/her information-seeking behavior and type one page about how they find and use information.
2. Keep an information need log for the coming week: each day, write down any instances when you needed information, and where you looked to get the information. This assignment can be neatly handwritten.
3. Choose a topic and list 3 questions you want to answer about it. **E-mail this to me before class on October 29.**
4. Reading: **Information Anxiety 2**, **Chapter 2** (pages 23 to 52). Do the accompanying writing assignment.
5. Notify me if you have selected the final presentation or teaching session (see page 4 of syllabus)

October 29/Class 2:
Research process: selecting a topic and formulating a thesis statement; methods of finding and accessing information, including the online catalog and classification systems
Introduction to the University Library
Reference sources
Style guides and citation format
Annotation format
Assignment: **Due at beginning of Class 3**
1. For the annotated bibliography, identify two books and two reference books on your topic. Type the citations for both, but annotate only the better of each pair.
2. Complete the Research Strategy worksheet: thesis statement, major concepts, synonyms and related terms.
3. Reading: *Research Strategies* text available through E-Reserves in Jacobson's folder: Chapter 1, Taking Charge. Do the accompanying writing assignment.
4. Readings: *Fishing for Information?* and *Checklist of Internet Research Tips* available at http://library.albany.edu/internet/checklist.html or through E-Reserves in Jacobson's folder.

November 5/Class 3:
Web search engines and structure
Effective Web search strategies
Evaluation of Web- and print-based information
Assignment: **Due at the beginning of Class 4**
1. Identify and cite one scholarly and one popular Web site on your topic. Annotate both of them. Attach the first page of each of the

Figure 3-4 continued

two sites.

2. For **each** of the two Web sites, fill out a Web Evaluation worksheet.
3. Reading: *Research Strategies* text available through E-Reserves in Jacobson's folder: Chapter 2, Databases. Do the accompanying writing assignment.

November 12/Class 4:

Periodicals: scholarly journals, popular magazines, newspapers
Finding articles: older vs. newer
Electronic databases: selection; search strategies: Boolean operators, fields, controlled vocabulary
Comparison of databases and the Web

Assignment: **Due at the beginning of Class 5**

1. For the annotated bibliography, hand in the first page of three articles on your topic: one must be from a popular or general **print** source (this can be a magazine or newspaper); one must be from a scholarly **print** source; and the third must be from an **online** full-text journal or magazine (you can use databases such as EBSCO, Expanded Academic Index, and LexisNexis, or electronic journal collections such as JSTOR or Science Direct to find online full-text articles). Also turn in the citations and annotations for all three articles.
2. Optional: Complete all three TILT modules and provide me with quiz results if you would like extra credit.

November 19/Class 5:

Flow of information
Primary and secondary sources
Information in the disciplines

Assignment: **Due at the beginning of Class 6**

1. Identify one primary and one secondary source on your topic, cite and annotate.
2. Identify one additional resource: an electronic reference source, a government document, or a multimedia source (this can be a video or audio clip mounted on the Web), cite and annotate.
3. Vocabulary worksheet.
4. Reading: The article distributed to you. Bring it to class 6.

December 3/Class 6:

Information ethics: copyright, plagiarism, privacy issues, digital divide
Course evaluation

Assignment: **Annotated bibliography due at the beginning of Class 7**

1. Complete the **10 item** annotated bibliography. (See pages 3–4 for the correct format.)
2. Prepare for and write an outline of the presentation to be turned in.

December 10/Class 7:

Review of course objectives
Post-test

Figure 3-4 continued

Five minute class presentations (see page 4 for more details)
Assignment: **Due at beginning of** *this* **class**

1. Annotated Bibliography due at beginning of this class.

2. Outline for your presentation.

Characteristics of *all* General Education Courses
1. General Education courses offer introductions to the central topics of disciplines and interdisciplinary fields.
2. General Education courses offer explicit rather than tacit understandings of the procedures, practices, methodology and fundamental assumptions of disciplines and interdisciplinary fields.
3. General Education courses recognize multiple perspectives on the subject matter.
4. General Education courses emphasize active learning in an engaged environment that enables students to be producers as well as consumers of knowledge.
5. General Education courses promote critical inquiry into the assumptions, goals, and methods of various fields of academic study; they aim to develop the interpretive, analytic, and evaluative competencies characteristic of critical thinking.

Information Literacy General Education Courses

Information Literacy General Education courses introduce students to various ways in which information is organized and structured and to the process of finding, using, producing, and distributing information in a variety of media formats, including traditional print as well as computer databases. Students acquire experience with resources available on the Internet and learn to evaluate the quality of information, to use information ethically and professionally, and to adjust to rapidly changing technology tools. Student must complete this requirement within the freshman or sophomore year.

Learning Objectives for General Education Information Literacy Courses

Courses in the category of Information Literacy will enable students to:

1. Locate, evaluate, synthesize and use information from a variety of sources
2. Understand and use basic research techniques appropriate to the course
3. Understand the various ways in which information is organized and structured
4. Understand the ethical issues involved in accessing and using information

Rev. 9/02/03

Figure 3-4 continued

First Day of Class

The first day of class is the time to capture students' attention. Compare the two scenarios in Figure 3–5.

First Day of Class	Alternate First Day of Class
It is the first day of class. You have a lot to cover and you have to let the students know everything you expect of them. Begin by reading over the syllabus in detail, so students will understand what exactly the course is, what their assignments will be, how many quizzes or tests they will have, and what the course policies are. Take attendance. Start with the first subject on the syllabus. At the end of the class, remind them that there will be a quiz next week on the material.	You have a lot you would like to accomplish on this first day. As students arrive in the room, provide them with copies of the syllabus. Chat with the early arrivals, and start learning their names. When it is time to start, introduce yourself to the students, and explain a bit about the course and why you teach it. Ask the students to pair up with someone they don't know, learn a little about each other (provide a question sheet to facilitate this) and then introduce their partner to the rest of the class. Ask the students why they are taking the class and what they hope to learn. Show the short video *E-literate?* which raises a number of information literacy issues. Hold a discussion about the video. Review important points in the syllabus and emphasize these elements that you included specifically for motivational purposes. Ask students what questions they have. Take a break. After the break, review the topics to be learned that day. After introducing the concepts of data, information, and knowledge, ask students to work in small groups to find an instance of each in a section of *The New York Times*.

Figure 3–5 Two Possible First Days of Class

These two scenarios are obviously written in such a way as to exaggerate the differences between them. But even experienced teachers, facing teaching a credit course for the first time, can slip into the types of behaviors and activities described in scenario number one, just through nervousness and inexperience with a protracted teaching experience, where you are the teacher rather than a guest lecturer. One of the authors found herself doing something close to what is described in the first scenario, until she realized this model was doing nothing to engage students in what was to come. Indeed, she was lucky that only some of the students were turned off by the end of the first class. The second scenario clearly needs more than an hour; however, it is very much possible to focus on student engagement in a shorter class than the one outlined.

Even on the first day, use a variety of teaching techniques. This is particularly important if you have a long class period (the alternate first day of class example is based on one two-hours long), but also applies in a 50- or 55-minute class. The video mentioned, *E-literate?* (2000), appeals to students, in that it is visual, full of action, and portrays college students in typical situations. It addresses many of the issues covered in an information literacy course, and hence serves as an excellent introduction to the topics in a more engaging manner than simply listing them. It also generates discussion, something that can be hard to induce on the first day of class.

In order to engage students actively throughout a course, it is critical to set the pattern on the first day of class. The video is one way to facilitate student discussion, but also plan for small group work, perhaps with group reports. This helps students begin to get comfortable with each other immediately (especially important for courses that only meet a small number of times). Build relevance into any such exercise and into all other elements of the first day. This can be done through making connections to other courses ("You can do your annotated bibliography on the same topic on which you are writing a paper, saving a great deal of time."), to their continued studies ("Seniors who have taken this course said that they wished they had taken it earlier in their academic career, it would have made research for so many courses much easier," and "This will help you immensely in graduate school."), and to their life outside of college ("Employers are looking for employees who are adept at doing research in this information-rich world.").

The first day of class is the first time you will meet your students; and the first impression that you and your course make upon them is critical. In order to begin motivating students from the start, and to continue to do so throughout the course, consider the elements that enhance student motivation from the minute you begin planning for the course.

ARCS Motivation Model and Initial Course Design

This chapter addresses six elements connected with the initial design of an information literacy course; although, several of the elements, such as topics, goals and objectives, and methods of instruction are critical considerations for all types of instruction. All of the elements tie closely to Keller's ARCS Motivation Model, most particularly to attention.

You should carefully consider the topics you select for a class, whether it is for an entire course or for a single time you will meet with a group of students, so that they capture student interest. It is also important for topics to be relevant to their needs as researchers. If you can connect the topics to their lives and experiences, they will find them even more relevant, and hence, motivating.

Relevance is critically important for the goals and objectives for a course or a single class, just as it is for topics. Do not stop with making links between your instruction and courses the students are currently taking. Strive to highlight connections between the material you are teaching and the lives and future plans of students, be they graduate school or the workplace. Your goals and objectives also provide a means for students to become more confident about their information literacy skills. Challenge students, but also make sure that you include areas in which students can succeed. If you provide opportunities for students to share their own knowledge, it will help them gain confidence.

Carefully designed instructional methods and assignments allow you to capture student interest, to stimulate their curiosity, and to enhance their confidence and satisfaction levels. We address this issue more fully in Chapter 5.

If you are teaching a full course, use the syllabus, as a representation of the course itself, to motivate your students in a number of ways. Highlight those elements of the course that you designed specifically to increase motivation — this will immediately capture students' attention. Use the syllabus to emphasize factors that students will find particularly relevant (such as the professional skills students will learn). The syllabus can be designed to increase every student's confidence to succeed. Evaluative criteria help them to understand just what is expected from them. Information about extra credit opportunities allows students more control over their performance in the class.

Every instructor should carefully design the first day of a course to capture the attention of each student. It is very important to motivate students right from the beginning, since it can be difficult to recapture the enthusiasm of students who have lost interest.

With all the tools at your disposal, you can do a lot to motivate students during the actual instruction, but do not neglect these six underpinning elements when planning for motivating students.

References

Gray, Peter. 1993. Engaging Students' Intellects: The Immersion Approach to Critical Thinking in Psychology Instruction. *Teaching of Psychology* 20, no. 2 (April): 68–74.

Keller, John M. 1987. Strategies for Stimulating the Motivation to Learn. *Performance & Instruction* 26, no. 8 (October): 1–7.

King, Angelynn. 2001. City Council Lab. In *Teaching Information Literacy Concepts: Activities and Frameworks from the Field*, edited by Trudi E. Jacobson and Timothy H. Gatti, 267–268. Pittsburgh: Library Instruction Publications.

Lowman, Joseph. 1995. *Mastering the Techniques of Teaching*. 2d ed. San Francisco: Jossey-Bass.

Pacific Bell and the UCLA Graduate School of Education and Information Studies. 2000. *E-literate?* 9 min. videocassette. Produced and Directed by Pacific Bell and the UCLA Graduate School of Education and Information Studies.

Chapter 4
Better Teaching Behaviors

Whether you are conducting a library tour or teaching a credit-based information literacy class, whether or not you are aware of it, you always exhibit certain behaviors in front of your students; for example, your voice level, facial expressions, and all the gestures you use to communicate. These behaviors have a strong effect on students: their attitude toward you, the class, and learning in general.

Think about the teachers or presenters you have experienced in the past. How did you feel when you had a bad teacher/presenter? You probably dozed off or walked out if you could. However, when you learned from a good teacher, you probably became totally absorbed in what was going on, got excited about what you were hearing, and felt that time went by quickly. What qualities do good teachers/presenters have in common? Passion, charisma, knowledge, good organization, clarity; and the list can go on.

Such terms often appear on student evaluation forms, and researchers have found that responses related to Enthusiasm/Expressiveness, Clarity of Explanation, and Rapport/Interaction are the strong predictors of instructional outcome, including teaching effectiveness and student achievement (Murray, 1997: 188). While good teaching behaviors promote student motivation and encourage them to learn, negative things teachers do in the classroom can dampen student enthusiasm. Behaviors such as poor presentation skills and lack of enthusiasm and organization contribute highly to demotivating students (Gorham and Millette, 1997: 257).

In this chapter, we discuss three teaching behaviors that directly affect student motivation:

- Enthusiasm
- Clarity/organization
- Interaction

Enthusiasm

What are you like when you are excited or enthusiastic about something? Can you sit or stand still? Do you raise your voice? And do you smile or laugh? If you are excited about teaching, you'll exhibit similar behaviors. Several behaviors reflect a teacher's enthusiasm:

- Speaking with vocal variety and quality
- Gesturing with hands and arms
- Moving around
- Maintaining eye contact
- Showing facial expressions

These behaviors serve to attract and hold student attention, the first motivation requirement in the ARCS Model.

Students often regard library classes as boring and not stimulating, but it does not have to be that way. You, as the instructor, can change that through the energy and enthusiasm you bring to the classroom. Enthusiasm is contagious. If you are enthusiastic about what you are doing, students will pay attention and become interested in the subject or material presented. Studies have shown that teacher enthusiasm is the most powerful predictor of student intrinsic motivation (Patrick, Hisley, and Kempler, 2000: 217). Students develop higher levels of motivation when they perceive their teachers are more enthusiastic (Christophel, 1990: 325).

After conducting the library tour or teaching the same topics many times, you might find yourself becoming less energetic; to you, it's just another class to teach. When you carry that feeling into the class, no matter how subtle it is, students can detect it and your attitude will immediately affect them. In response, students will become bored and restless. To avoid losing your enthusiasm, talk to your colleagues and try new things (including teaching methods) once in a while.

Speaking with Vocal Variety and Quality

It is common sense that when you teach, you should project your voice and at least make it audible (though not deafening). You might want to ask if everybody, particularly those in the back, can hear you. Although it is a little gesture, it shows that you care. Meanwhile, strive for vocal variety and quality.

Your voice reflects the level of engagement you have in the material, as well as the enjoyment you feel toward teaching (Nilson, 1998: 46). A monotone or dull voice is not only dreadful to listen to, but also boring.

Before long, a student's mind and attention can drift away from the class and what you are trying to teach. On the contrary, "[a] speaker whose voice is sometimes loud, sometimes soft, sometimes fast, sometimes slow, sometimes sharp and crisp, and sometimes mellow and melodic is more likely to keep an audience's attention than one whose voice has any one quality for too long" (Lowman, 1995: 109).

Gesturing and Moving Around

As Keller suggests, "any sudden or unexpected change in the environment will activate a person's attention" (1987: 2). Your voice level, gestures, and movement have this kind of effect on students. "The Statue" who never moves away from the podium where he or she is stationed, who reads directly from the text, and who never looks at the students can very easily cause boredom in students; on the other hand, "The Acrobat," who, with wild antics, charges over the entire classroom can also distract students from what he or she is trying to convey in class (LaGuardia and Oka, 2000: 14–16).

How much you can move around depends on how comfortable you feel, as well as the nature of the class, and the physical constraints of the classroom. Not everyone is comfortable with the idea of walking around the room. To begin with, you can stay at the podium if you face all students, but make sure you use plenty of gestures to accompany your speech and maintain constant eye contact with your students. Once you are comfortable, then try to move away from the podium once in a while. When you stand, be sure to have your shoulders back, head erect, and eyes looking directly at the students' faces, because, "slumped-over posture and avoidance of eye contact communicate uncertainty and discomfort" (Lowman, 1995: 106).

The classroom where we teach UNL205 has the computers set against the walls, and the instructor podium in the middle of the room with a pillar right next to it. Wherever we stand, we cannot see all our students at once, because of the pillar and because some students are actually behind us. When we teach, we move away from the podium and walk around; thus, we're able to see all of the students during the class, and we become visible to all of them. This way, nobody is able to hide safely in the corner or behind us. When we move around, we find that the eyes of the students follow us. Those sitting in the corner or behind us are pleased that we notice them and speak to them, and they participate more actively in class.

Maintaining Eye Contact

Whatever you do, make sure you keep eye contact with your students. Your eye contact "personalizes your comments, encourages students to return your attentiveness to them in kind, and enables you to 'read their faces' to gauge their interest and understanding" (Nilson, 1998: 46). Looking directly at students might be uncomfortable, difficult, as well as discouraging, especially when are you are nervous and find students not paying attention.

LaGuardia and Oka suggest using the forehead gaze technique as a start-up trick.

**Figure 4-1 Instructor Tip:
The Forehead Gaze Technique**

Let your gaze move over [the] entire class, looking NO ONE in the eye. Instead, direct your gaze at the point on their foreheads between their eyebrows. Start with one side of the room and move your gaze over the whole class, one at a time, or picking out individuals in various rows at various times: but don't look anybody in the eye. Look at foreheads.

(LaGuardia and Oka, 2000: 15)

After you become comfortable in the classroom, then look directly into the eyes of students. Your eye contact with students should be long enough to pique their interest. Nilson suggests three seconds per student (1998: 46). When a student answers, listen and look, don't avoid their eyes, this will show them your intense interest in their comments. When you see confused or blank faces, you should change your instruction pace and clarify the points you just covered, to get and hold their attention once more.

Class Notes

You probably have notes with you when you go to teach. It is a good idea to have notes handy; because, no matter how well prepared you are, sometimes your mind goes blank. The notes you bring to the classroom can release you from this kind of awkwardness and serve to remind you of the important points you intend to cover. However, do not rely too much on your notes. Don't read from the notes or ruffle through them to find what you cannot seem to remember. This will make you "lose spontaneity, expressiveness, flexibility, eye contact, and most importantly psychological contact with the class, lulling students into a passive, even inattentive state of mind" (Nilson, 1998: 80). Students will lose confidence in you, since they see it as a sign of your own lack of confidence. (See Figure 4-2)

In addition, no matter how well you have prepared the class and how many times you have taught the same topics, teach it as if you were doing it the first time. "[T]he actual delivery should have a sense of immediacy," because "this quality of conversational intimacy involves the students more readily in the flow of ideas than does a didactic style" (Lowman, 1995: 141).

Figure 4-2 Instructor Tip:
Class Notes

When you started to teach, you might have spent a lot of time preparing and had lengthy notes for each class. You might still spend a lot of time on class preparation, but your notes may have become much shorter. Part of the reason is that over time you have learned the subject by heart, and part of it is that you've probably found it's better not to use very detailed notes. Type up your notes in a big font on the top half of the paper. This way, when you need to consult the notes, you only have to glance at the paper quickly to find out what is there.

Showing Facial Expressions

Other than your voice and physical movement, your face also indicates how you feel about the subject and about teaching. Instead of a glazed look and blank face, an enthusiastic teacher has animated facial expressions. But when you are nervous, you might be at a loss for what to do and how to behave. Like us, you may have wondered how you should appear in front of your students. Should you bear a stern face or smile at them? How should you respond to students? LaGuardia and Oka suggest trying out five safe and neutral expressions before your stage fright passes.

Safe and Neutral Expressions

- Calm blandness
- Interested concern
- Thoughtful consideration
- Eager anticipation
- Smiling affability

Figure 4–3 Safe and Neutral Expressions
(LaGuardia and Oka, 2000: 22)

This might not work for everybody, and some might not be comfortable with such an idea. If not, then find expressions with which you are comfortable. Keep in mind, whatever you do, the most important thing is to be yourself and to be sincere.

Clarity

Lowman suggests that the clarity of an instructor's presentation can help create intellectual excitement in students, while confusing presentations can dampen students' curiosity and desire to seek challenges (1995: 21, 55). For the presentation to be clear, the instructor should have

- a thorough knowledge of the topic;
- the ability to see to the heart of the matter;
- the ability to see it from the learners' perspective; and
- the ability to explain it simply (Sotto, 1994: 126).

Translated into concrete and detectable teaching behaviors, this means several things:

- Speaking clearly
- Presenting clearly
- Using an outline
- Focusing on major points
- Illustrating with examples
- Using visuals
- Reviewing and summarizing

Such behaviors meet three of Keller's four motivation conditions: attention, relevance, and confidence.

Speaking Clearly

In the previous section, we suggested that you speak with vocal variety and quality. To hold student attention, you also need to speak clearly. No matter what you are trying to present or how passionate you feel about it, if your speech is not clear, students will not be able to

Figure 4–4 Instructor Tip: Speech Clarity

You might not be aware of your own speech habits, since they are so automatic by now, it takes some real effort even to notice them. You can tape your own presentation, or better yet, have it taped and review it later, or ask a colleague to sit in your class to observe and to give you feedback. This will help you realize what you are doing wrong so you can correct it.

understand what you are talking about, and most likely they will not pay any attention. Mannerisms, such as "Um," "Uh," "You know," "sort of," and "kind of," as well as redundancy of words, false starts, stutters, mispronunciations, and mumbles, can distract students from the actual content (Lowman, 1995: 103–104; Nilson, 1998: 46), and cause "students to lose confidence in the instructor and thus in themselves" (Murray, 1997: 193). You should minimize or eliminate such distracting speech habits.

Presenting Clearly

It is probably safe to assume that we all are knowledgeable about what we teach. Students are not as knowledgeable, and that is the reason why most of them are in the classroom. What makes good sense to you, an expert of the field, might not resonate well with your students; therefore, to make your presentation clear, you need to approach and organize the subject matter and present it from the student's perspective. You should "focus on the early observations, essential milestones, key assumptions, and critical insights in a subject," and "explain ideas and the connections between them in ways that make eminently good sense to the [students]" (Lowman, 1995: 22–23). Regardless of the topic, you should explain it in simple and plain language, so that students can understand what is going on and follow your leads. Jargon can only cause confusion in students and should be avoided where possible.

Using an Outline

When students are not sure what topics you intend to cover in class and what you expect them to do, they lack a sense of control and can become frustrated (Lowman, 1995: 55). To solve this problem, explain to students verbally what you hope to cover in class and what you expect of them, or provide an outline on the board, on an overhead, or in a handout. The outline highlights the topics and your major points, and serves to structure the class. It "will ensure that students are following your logical flow, especially if you occasionally refer to it to point out your location in the lecture" (Nilson, 1998: 79).

For each class, develop a one-page outline and project it on the screen or distribute it to the class. Lay out each topic and list two or three major points for each. Under each major point, list related important ideas, but do not include more than three layers. Figure 4–5 is a sample outline for an early class in which we discuss the research process, introduce reference sources, and explain how to use the catalog to search for reference materials.

Class Outline

1. Research Process
   • Thesis Statement
      Research Question
   • Reference Sources
      Types
2. Online Catalog
   • Exact Searching
      Title
      Author
      Subject
   • Keyword Searching
3. Annotated Bibliography
   • Bibliography
      Citations: MLA Style
   • Annotations
      Elements
   • Annotated Bibliography Format

Figure 4–5 Class Outline

Focusing on Major Points

You have probably found yourself in the situation of having too much to cover during too limited time, especially when you are asked to teach a one-shot session, and the professor has told you specifically to include everything in the session. What should you do? Should you squeeze as much content as possible into the short time you have?

You might find it hard to resist such an urge, but your attempt to cover too much material will not only result in the superficial coverage of each point, but also a rushed delivery pace (Lowman, 1995: 136). Students need time to process the information they receive and think about what is presented to them. Too much information coming too quickly can only overwhelm and confuse them, and they will "often tune out" (Erickson and Strommer, 1991: 97). To avoid swamping students and to make the class more productive, you need to concentrate on essential topics and points.

Use the following four criteria to help you decide what to present:

• Present central points or general themes that tie together as many other topics as possible.
• Select points for their high interest to students.
• Occasionally choose an especially difficult topic.
• Choose a topic based on its depth and complexity; make sure it's neither too difficult nor too simplistic (Lowman, 1995: 137–138).

Regardless of the length of your information literacy class, you probably find that the time you have is far from adequate to cover what you would like to teach. Revise the syllabus every semester to weed out the nonessential material, and do the same thing with the content of each class. Instead of spreading class time too thinly to include everything you would like to teach, focus on the most important topics, such as evaluating information and its sources, and developing sound search strategies. Try to connect as many class topics together as you can. Figure 4–6 is an example of what we are doing with our information literacy course.

Exercise Example: Improving Electronic Database Search Results

Figure 4–6 Instructor Tip: Major Points
The topic of information evaluation is introduced in the first class and is emphasized throughout the course. During the first or second class, each student is asked to evaluate a sample article and write a critical annotation of it. Starting with the second or third class, students start to work on their own annotated bibliography project, which requires them to not only look for information but also evaluate what they have found. Database searching strategies is another important topic, which we discuss in class three or four. Before the class, students are assigned to read Chapter 2, Databases, in *Research Strategies* by William Badke. During class, we spend a great deal of time explaining the three Boolean operators—first we ask students to draw diagrams and then ask them to do searches to see how each operator affects the search results. After class, each student is assigned to complete the *Researching 101* online tutorial. The tutorial allows them to review what they have learned about the three Boolean operators, the online catalog (discussed in the previous class), the differences between keyword and subject searching, and how to choose the best materials and most appropriate databases. During the ensuing class, students are paired up to work on the Improving Your Search Results worksheet (see figure 4–7).

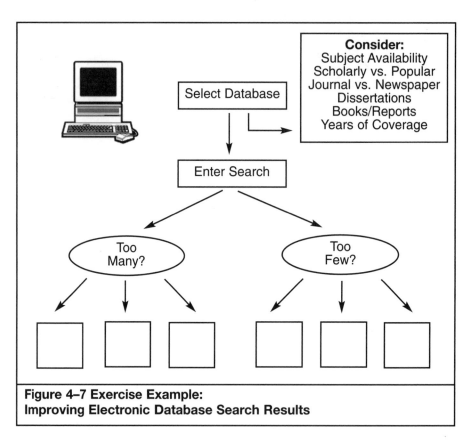

Figure 4–7 Exercise Example:
Improving Electronic Database Search Results

Illustrating with Examples

To make your points clear, you should illustrate freely. "People are more interested in the concrete than the abstract, and in real people and events rather than humanity in general or hypothetical events" (Keller, 1983: 402). Abstract and dry theory often confuses and turns away students. To keep their attention and maintain their curiosity, you need to follow a theoretical point with practical examples (Sotto, 1994: 126). Such examples link the new concept with the prior knowledge of the students, the unfamiliar and abstract with the familiar and concrete. They clarify your point and help students better understand the material. The connection also helps students retain and remember the information. Draw examples from settings familiar to students, to which they can easily relate. Examples should be striking, vivid, current, and common in everyday life (Nilson, 1998: 79).

When discussing copyright, ask students to look up definitions on the Internet for these terms: copyright, intellectual property, fair use, and public domain. This helps students gain some basic knowledge about copyright and its related issues before the class discussion. It also gives students a chance to use what they have learned from previous class: Internet search tools and strategies. After the search exercise, briefly discuss these terms and copyright periods. Then divide students into groups and assign each group a case (see Figure 4–7). Hold class discussion after students complete group work and group discussions.

Exercise Example: Copyright

Case #1
You are surfing the Web one day and come across this really cool picture that would be perfect for your Web site. There is no copyright notice on the Web site, so you save a copy of the picture and put it up on your Web site, A couple of weeks later you get an e-mail message from someone claiming you violated their copyright by doing this. Did you? Why/why not?

Case #2
You write an article that gets accepted for publication in one of the student publications on your campus. Before you publish your article, you sign a piece of paper transferring copyright to the publisher. Is it okay for you to put a copy of the article on your own Web site? Why/why not?

Case #3
Honored with an award for community service, the presenter asks you to give a speech. You didn't even know you had been nominated, and you haven't prepared anything. You give a speech off the top of your head, and it is incredibly thoughtful, insightful, and "together." One of your peers sitting in the audience copies down a large portion of your speech without your knowledge and uses several lines from your speech two weeks later in a speech of her own. Did she violate copyright? Why/why not?

**Figure 4–8 Exercise Example: Copyright
(Adapted from Bell, 2001: 223)**

Using Visuals

In addition to examples, visual aids such as pictures, slides, diagrams, concept maps, power point, and videos help illustrate content clearly and vividly. As Erickson and Strommer point out, people process information better and faster through the eye than the ear, and playing to both of these senses can increase attention, as well as

---

Figure 4–9 Instructor Tip: Visuals

When discussing the research process, you can start by asking how students feel toward their research project. Then pair the students up, and ask them to draw a process diagram together. After five minutes or so, convene the class, ask them for the steps they developed, and draw a diagram together with the students. When introducing primary and secondary sources, you can use a PowerPoint presentation; when discussing Web evaluation, you can use a video. Visuals don't have to be fancy. Utilize what is available to you. Vary the visuals you use; the variety helps keep students interested.

---

facilitate explanation and learning (1991: 101). Students also come with different learning styles, and the use of visual aids is critical for those with a visual learning style (Nilson, 1998: 79; see Figure 4-9).

During the presentation, it is a good idea to write down the new concepts or terms or key points you are introducing on a flip chart, or display them on the overhead screen. You can also write down student responses. The process of writing during lecture can help direct the attention of students and focus it on what is going on in class (Lowman, 1995: 146).

Reviewing and Summarizing

Key ideas and difficult points are clear to us, but they might not be to the students. Therefore, you should stress and repeat these points throughout the class. To do this, periodically review at the end of each section, and summarize at the end of the class. Reviewing at the end of each section also signals the transition from one topic to another. "By providing clear cues marking the end of one topic and the beginning of another, teachers can help to keep students from getting confused and help them to follow the transition" (Jacobson and Xu, 2002: 430).

Instead of teaching to the absolute last minute, always set aside several minutes for the end of the class recap activities. You can summarize what you covered in the class, or even better ask students to do it. The recap activities may take the form of an oral summary or classroom assessment technique, such as a one-minute paper. For example, you can ask students to write down the most important points or confusing points of the class. Such activities encourage students to collect their own thoughts, make material meaningful by restating it in their own language, and help them to remember the information (Erickson and Strommer, 1991: 106, 67). The summary can also highlight for you what they do or do not understand, and you can follow up to clarify and repeat what they have not understood.

Interaction

When you step into a classroom to teach, you are communicating more than just the contents of the class. The way you teach and communicate also show the kind of person you are, and how you feel about your students (Sotto, 1994: 150). You can stir up negative emotions in students, such as anger, anxiety, and resentment, if you disrespect, ridicule, or treat them unfairly. Positive emotions, such as respect, confidence, security, and trust, can be generated or promoted through the respect and confidence you show toward them. These two sets of classroom emotions strongly influence student motivation: the former dims students' desire to learn while the latter increases their motivation (Lowman, 1995: 27–28). To motivate students, you need to avoid stimulating negative feelings and do what you can to remove fear and anxiety from the classroom (Keller, 1987: 4).

The following teaching behaviors can help create interpersonal rapport and a positive learning environment:

- Getting to know students and addressing them by name
- Asking questions
- Encouraging questions and comments
- Praising freely and dealing with mistakes tactfully
- Assuming equality
- Employing a variety of activities and teaching techniques

Classroom interaction behaviors are closely related to the ARCS Model, especially to relevance, confidence, and satisfaction.

Getting to Know Students and Addressing Them by Name

Getting to know students, finding out their majors and background, and addressing them by name all indicate your strong personal interest in them. Your personal interest in the students, "will inspire their personal loyalty to you" (Nilson, 1998: 58). The simplest and easiest way to start to know your students is through class introductions: have students introduce themselves.

Before you meet with the students for the first time, review the class roster to familiarize yourself with their names. During the first class, hand out an introduction form (see figure 4–9). Have student fill out the form and then introduce themselves, or pair them up to interview and introduce each other to the entire class.

Introduction Form

Name:

E-mail address:

Phone number:

What city/town/country are you from?

What is your major (if you've already picked one)?

Favorite movie(s):

Favorite book(s):

Hobbies:

What are your experiences with computers?

_____Word processing

_____PowerPoint

_____Spread sheet

_____Programming

_____E-mail

_____Internet

_____Others:

Anything else about you:

What would you like to learn from this class?

Any other expectations for the class:

Figure 4–10 Introduction Form

Such introductions help you to learn more about your students, and at the same time shows students that you care about who they are and how they feel about the class. It also gives you a chance to connect the names on the roster with students' faces, which helps you to remember their names. Through the introduction you can also learn how their names are pronounced and what they prefer to be called.

> Don't forget to introduce yourself to the class. Before the student introductions, we tell students our names, background, interests, and other pertinent information. Students tend to follow our example. We have found that the more information we reveal to our students about ourselves, the more students will talk about themselves, when it comes to their turn to do the introduction.

Try to remember your students' names and start addressing them by name by the end of the first class meeting, or by the second class, at the latest. You might not be able to do so if you have a very large class, but start with a few and go from there. The results will amaze you. "[L]earning each student name is so effective at promoting rapport because it begins personal contact immediately but does not seem forced, rushed, or intrusive" (Lowman, 1995: 67).

The information collected on the form, such as their major and interests, is later incorporated into classes to make them more appealing. The introduction form often reveals useful information teachers would not otherwise be able to find out. For example, you might have students who write down that they have learning disabilities and indicate what kind of class they prefer. This will alert you to their needs and help you to design better classes.

Be sure to arrive at the classroom 10–15 minutes ahead of class time. This will give you time to check the classroom to make sure that everything, including the lights and computers, is all set for the class. When your students walk in, you can greet them and chat with them before class starts. You can find out more about your students and get to know them better this way.

Asking Questions

To keep students actively engaged in the class, it is essential to have them participate. When you pose a question in class, you are inviting your students to think, talk, and participate. Keep in mind that you are not using the questions to test students, rather, to initiate a discussion to clarify something. Students will speak most readily when they sense they will not be evaluated (Sotto, 1994: 151).

We have all had this kind of experience: we ask a question, the class goes quiet, and nobody responds. The silence seems to go on forever. Nothing is more dreadful than this kind of silence. To end it, we

---

Figure 4-11 Instructor Tip: Questioning Techniques

Word your questions clearly. Avoid asking questions that can be answered with short factual statements or with "Yes" or "No" responses. Avoid asking a second or third question immediately after the first question, as it will only confuse students. Ask questions in a relaxed and confident manner. When you finish, start counting silently to yourself, "one thousand and one, one thousand and two,"… to "one thousand and ten." Scan the room slowly, remaining calm and relaxed. When you finish the count, if nobody answers, remain clam. Repeat the question in a shorter and slightly modified form, and begin your silent count again.

Adapted from Lowman, 1995: 180–181

---

might feel attempted to fill it up by supplying answers ourselves. However, don't attempt to do so. Once you do it, it will get students into the habit of sitting passively and waiting for you to answer all of your own questions.

Be patient and don't get angry. If you set aside time to wait, they will answer.

Encouraging Students' Questions and Comments

Teaching is not the simple relay of information from the instructor to the students. It should foster communication in both directions (Nilson, 1998: 59). Ask students for feedback and comments and find out how they feel. This indicates your interest in their opinions, as well as their learning. You can do so by simply asking questions, such as, "Are there any questions?" or "Am I going too fast?" Lowman reminds us that "[o]ccasionally instigating feedback from students keeps them alert and lets them know the instructor is concerned" (1995: 144). In addition, you can also use in-class assessment techniques to solicit feedback from students. For example, at the end of the class, you can hand out index cards and ask students to write down the most confusing

---

Figure 4-12 Instructor Tip: Encouraging Questions and Comments

When students ask a question, if you don't understand or don't know anything about it, admit it. This helps students feel safe in doing the same (Billson and Tiberius, 1991: 104). However, don't stop here, tell the students you'll find out more about it after class and ask them to explore the issue too. During the next class, follow up with what you discover.

---

topic of the day, or to make suggestions about the class.

When students ask questions or make comments, don't cut them off. Never ridicule them or embarrass them. Acknowledge their comments. Don't attempt to answer all of the questions yourself, redirect the questions and ask other students to answer instead (Billson and Tiberius, 1991: 97). This method involves more than just the student and the teacher. It gives other students an opportunity to contribute and to share their ideas and thoughts with the rest of the class, which will make students feel more confident.

Such a process can also help students discover that their opinions, fears, or problems are not unique; consequently, they will less likely feel timid in the future to express themselves (Billson and Tiberius, 1991: 91).

Praising Students Freely and Pointing out Their Mistakes Tactfully

When students present a good idea or make a good point, you should compliment them with a nod or by saying "Excellent," "That's great," or "That's a very good point." Your praise acknowledges their opinions and conveys your respect toward the students, which makes them feel good about themselves and provides a sense of satisfaction. Consequently, they participate more actively in class and feel more inclined toward learning. (See Figure 4-13)

Figure 4-13 Instructor Tip: Praising
In addition to your verbal acknowledgement, you can praise students through other venues. If there is a project that a student does well, ask the student to share it with the rest of the class. For example, ask the student to do a sample search or show the class a good annotation he or she has written.

It's inevitable to make mistakes and we learn from our mistakes. We learn teaching this way — through the trial and error method. We need to be tolerant of student errors. This being said, it does not mean you should ignore an error when it occurs; but, how you deal with it has a tremendous effect on students. If you respond with blunt messages, such as, "This is completely wrong," "This is stupid," "No, it should be…" and laugh at it, you will not only embarrass them, but also make them feel foolish. As a result, they will turn away from the class and from learning. Instead, try to "foster a classroom climate in which learners feel able to make mistakes, can talk to each other about them, and hence learn from them" (Sotto, 1994: 125). You should deal with a mistake by asking the student to explain why he or she thinks that way, or by turning to the class and asking other students what they think about it. What other students say often carries more weight than your comments (Sotto, 1994: 123).

Assuming Equality

Teaching behaviors such as praising students for good ideas and asking them for feedback and comments make students feel good about themselves. On the other hand, appearing superior or snobbish in front of students can generate unnecessary fear and anxiety. Richmond's study shows that the use of authority- and coercion-based Behavior Alteration Techniques (e.g., reward, punishment, teacher authority) is negatively associated with student motivation (1990: 188–189).

Students often view the teacher as the authority in the classroom. Of course you need to exert some control over the class, so that it will take the direction you would like, and to avoid chaos. But, at the same time, you can also give students choices. Both students and the teacher must share the responsibility of the learning experience and its outcome. Students enjoy learning more if they have a sense of control over what is happening. Chapter 6, Student Autonomy, discusses how you can achieve this in the areas of course activity, content, policy, assignments, and student assessment. The proper use of verbal and body language can also help de-emphasize your role as an authority figure and lessen your controlling role.

> **Figure 4-14 Instructor Tip: Assuming Equality**
>
> Pay attention to the verbs you use in the classroom. Always include yourself as part of the class by referring to the class as "our class," "what we are doing," or "what we will do today." This shows your stake in the class. When asking students to do something, use expressions such as "I would like" instead of the ordering tones "I want" or "You should." Check your syllabus and make sure to eliminate these words.

When attempting to control students, suggesting and implying rather than ordering or directing...leads students to take responsibility for their own behavior—to become controlled from within...When announcing a course assignment, college teachers emphasize the formal dimension of their relationship with students when they say "I require," "I expect" or "You must." In contrast, saying "I would like," "It is my hope" or "You will probably want" emphasizes the instructor as person rather than authority. Using these words implies that the students will choose to do something because it is what they, or someone they like, want rather than because they have been coerced (Lowman, 1995: 74-75).

In addition, you should treat all students equally, and hold all of them to the same standards. Students come from different backgrounds and with various experiences. Some are obviously more motivated than others. It is natural for you to like a student more if he or she contributes a lot in the classroom or does well on every quiz and assignment. But any favoritism you show towards a student will only make the others feel you are being unfair, and such "[i]nequality in classroom interaction has a poisonous effect on trust" (Billson and Tiberius, 1991: 90). To promote equality and equity among students, Nilson has suggested the following guidelines:

- Give attention to all students as equally as possible.
- Praise them equally for equal quality responses.
- Use non-stereotypical examples.
- Use gender-neutral language.
- Resist falling into reverse discrimination by giving inordinate attention to minority and disabled students.
- Be sensitive to any difficulties students may have in understanding you (1998: 60).

Employing a Variety of Activities and Teaching Techniques

To keep student attention, the rule of thumb is never to do anything for too long (Lowman, 1995: 142). Regardless of what you teach, remember to introduce change and variety in your class.

> [Good teachers] engaged their learners in a wide variety of activities. This variety wasn't just in the content of the lesson. For example, they varied the challenges which they posed: first one kind of task, then another. They also varied the social configurations in the class: sometimes the learners worked individually, sometimes in groups, and sometimes the whole class worked together.... These teachers also varied the teaching/learning methods they used: sometimes the teacher talked, sometimes the learners talked to the teacher, sometimes the learners read, sometimes they wrote, sometimes they did practical things, and sometimes the learners discussed things in small groups. All in a purposeful and organized way (Sotto, 1994: 129).

To make your lecture more interactive, you can incorporate activities, such as group discussions, hands-on activities, and writing-to-learn exercises. These activities keep students' attention, engage them actively in the class, and help dispel boredom. In addition, injecting humor into the classroom not only lightens the mood, but it is also a

---

**Figure 4-15 Instructor Tip:
Variety of Activities**

Employ various activities and techniques in your classes. The format you use depends on the class. For example, during a class on information formats, first discuss the characteristics of periodicals by comparing them with books and reference books. To differentiate scholarly journals from popular magazines, form students into groups. Give each group one journal and one magazine. Ask them to find and list the differences between the two. After 10 minutes or so, convene the class and begin a class discussion. Then summarize the differences by giving students a handout and stress the major differences again. On the topic of periodical databases, cite an article from *Time* magazine (which was used in the comparison exercise), and ask each student to log into the online catalog to look for the article since students often confuse the catalog with the periodical databases. After students have exhausted title, author, subject, and keyword searches to look for the article, ask them to log into a database such as EBSCO to do a search. Before having further discussions on databases in general, ask students to pair up or work individually to complete a database worksheet (see Figure 6-10).

---

good way to introduce variety (Lowman, 1995: 143). But don't use it if you don't feel comfortable with it. More importantly, don't use it for the sake of the humor itself. Use it only in the context of what you are trying to teach. Visuals and vivid examples can make your presentation more interesting, as well. Vary the techniques and methods you use. Don't stick with one thing only. Try new ways. According to Keller, a sequence of a warm-up activity, a short lecture, a demonstration, and an exercise is excellent, but when it is used all the time without any change, it becomes predictable to students, and therefore boring (1987: 3).

Students have diverse backgrounds. The various activities and techniques you employ will make the class more appealing by catering to their different needs, knowledge levels, and learning styles. Hands-on activities provide practical application opportunities. They help students better understand what they have just learned and can boost their confidence, as well as satisfaction level. In Chapter 5, we will discuss three active engagement methods: cooperative learning, writing to learn, and discovery learning.

ARCS Motivation Model and Teaching Behaviors

As described earlier in this chapter, teacher enthusiasm behaviors convey your passion for the subject and for teaching, and students are likely affected by your attitude. It can ignite their interest in what you are presenting and their desire to learn. The changes in your voice level, facial expressions, and physical movement create motions in class; therefore, they help capture student attention. Enthusiasm behaviors also help build content relevance and confidence in students. "It takes an enthusiastic teacher to make students care about making choices, to provide a meaningful context for the materials in a course, to make students curious about those materials" (Beidler and Beidler, 1993: 21).

When a class is presented in a clear, understandable, and well organized manner, students will likely focus their attention on what is going on in class and follow your lead. Clarity of speech and presentation, the use of examples and visuals, and in class reviews all help students better understand the content. Highlighting major points, such as those of interest to students, make the material relevant to them. Presenting the material from the student's perspective, and using examples with which they are familiar, serve the same purpose.

Interaction behaviors such as encouraging students to participate in class not only keep them actively engaged, but also help achieve relevance through their participation. Since students come with diverse backgrounds, you can increase the relevance when you employ various activities and techniques. Confidence and satisfaction come into play when instructors offer students opportunities to practice and apply what they have learned, whether individually or in a group. Techniques such as asking students for opinions and comments show your respect for and confidence in the students, which help them become more confident.

References

Badke, William. 2000. Databases. In *Research Strategies*. Online. Available: www.acts.twu.ca/lbr/chapter2.htm (2003, August 18).

Beidler, Peter G., and Gretchen M. Beidler. 1993. What's Your Horse: Motivating College Students. *Journal on Excellence in College Teaching* 4: 9–26.

Bell, Colleen. 2001. From Ethics to Copyright Law: Protecting Intellectual Property in the 21st Century. In *Teaching Information Literacy Concepts: Activities and Frameworks from the Field*, edited by Trudi E. Jacobson and Timothy H. Gatti, 249–254. Pittsburgh: Library Instruction Publications.

Billson, Janet M., and Richard G. Tiberius. 1991. Effective Social Arrangements for Teaching and Learning. In *College Teaching: From Theory to Practice*, edited by Robert J. Menges and Marilla D. Svinicki. New Directions for Teaching and Learning, no. 45 (Spring): 87–109.

Christophel, Diane M. 1990. The Relationships Among Teacher Immediacy Behaviors, Students Motivation, and Learning. *Communication Education* 39 (October): 323–340.

Erdle, Stephen, and Harry G. Murray. 1986. Interfaculty Differences in Classroom Teaching Behaviors and Their Relationship to Student Instructional Ratings. *Research in Higher Education* 24, no. 2: 114–127.

Erickson, Bette L., and Diane W. Strommer. 1991. *Teaching College Freshmen*. San Francisco: Jossey-Bass.

Gorham, Joan, and Diane M. Millette. 1997. A Comparative Analysis of Teacher and Student Perceptions of Sources of Motivation and Demotivation in College Classes. *Communication Education* 46 (October): 245–261.

Jacobson, Trudi E., and Carol Anne Germain. 2000. Researching 101. Online. Available: http://library.albany.edu/usered/tutdex/index.html (2003, August 18).

Jacobson, Trudi E., and Lijuan Xu. 2002. Motivating Students in Credit-based Information Literacy Courses: Theories and Practice. *portal: Libraries and the Academy* 2, no. 3 (July): 423–441.

Keller, John M. 1983. Motivational Design of Instruction. In *Instructional-design Theories & Models: An Overview of Their Current Status*, edited by Charles M. Reigeluth, 383–434. Hillsdale, NJ: Lawrence Erlbaum Associates.

– – –. 1987. Strategies for Stimulating the Motivation to Learn. *Performance and Instruction* 26, no. 8 (October): 1– 7.

LaGuardia, Cheryl, and Christine K. Oka. 2000. *Becoming a Library Teacher*. New York: Neal-Schuman.

Lowman, Joseph. 1995. *Mastering the Techniques of Teaching*. 2d ed. San Francisco: Jossey-Bass.

Murray, Harry G. 1997. Effective Teaching Behaviors in the College Classroom. In *Effective Teaching in Higher Education*, edited by Raymond P. Perry and John Smart, 171–204. New York: Agathon Press.

Nilson, Linda B. 1998. *Teaching at Its Best: A Research Based Resource for College Instructors*. Bolton, MA: Anker Publishing.

Patrick, Brian C., Jennifer Hisley, and Toni Kempler. 2000. "What's Everybody So Excited About?": The Effects of Teacher Enthusiasm on Student Intrinsic Motivation and Vitality. *The Journal of Experimental Education* 68, no. 3 (Spring): 217–236.

Richmond, Virginia P. 1990. Communication in the Classroom: Power and Motivation. *Communication Education* 39 (July): 181–195.

Sotto, Eric. 1994. *When Teaching Becomes Learning: A Theory and Practice of Teaching*. London: Cassell.

Chapter 5
Active Learning Techniques

D o you remember how you learned to drive? Did you read about it or have someone give you a few lectures on it, and then leap into the car to take a road trip? Or did you learn by trying it out? While some people do learn well by reading and listening, many more need to try something out, to practice, before they become adept. This applies to skills related to information literacy, as much as it does to driving a car, or cooking, or flying a kite.

Librarians who teach have all heard about the empty vessel theory of teaching: students are empty vessels, and you just pour into their heads what you want them to know; or the sponge theory, where they will absorb what you teach. However, students are neither empty vessels, nor sponges. They come complete with knowledge and experiences of their own, and they do not simply replace what they know with what you teach them. They need a chance to compare what they know with what they are learning, figure out how the pieces interrelate, and come up with a new knowledge set. In order to do this effectively, they need to interact more closely with the course material than simply listening to it or reading about it. They need to do something active with it: talk about it with classmates, try it out, make mistakes and see what needs fixing, try again.

Active Learning in the Classroom

Active learning and teaching methods, of which there are numerous permutations, enable students to interact more closely with course material. Many librarians teaching information literacy courses already use a variety of these methods. Not only do these techniques encourage more effective learning on the part of students, but they also can be extremely effective in motivating students. They rank high on all four of Keller's elements: attention, relevance, confidence, and satisfaction. Engaging students very directly in the learning process does get their attention. If you develop the active learning activities well and gear them to the appropriate level, students will find them relevant. If students do well in the activities, their confidence is bolstered, and they feel a sense of satisfaction at what they have been able to accomplish.

Researchers have found that students who learn something in order to teach others, rather than in preparation for a test, have enhanced intrinsic motivation and enhanced learning (Benware and Deci, 1984). While we may not have the freedom to set up our courses to allow students to learn solely to teach others, this is one type of active learning we can use from time to time.

Students can engage in some of these active learning methods individually, while other activities are designed for groups of learners, as shown in Figure 5-1. Having a variety of these methods at your fingertips allows flexibility, not only for the subject matter, but also for the size of the class.

Active Learning Methods for Individuals and Groups

Methods that can be done by individuals
- Solve problems
- Apply general principles to real-world examples
- Record reactions to readings or presentations in journals

Methods that can be done in groups
- Solve problems
- Small group work
- Participation in simulations
- Group presentations
- Small group debates
- Cooperative projects

Figure 5–1 Active Learning Methods for Individuals and Groups (Adapted from Lowman, 1995: 204.)

Additional research shows that students become more engaged in learning situations where they work together, with a focus on individual improvement, gaining new skills, challenge, and where the instructor de-emphasizes grades or performance factors, such as comparison between students' work (Karabenick and Collins-Eaglin, 1997).

We can group active learning methods into different categories. This chapter considers characteristics of each of the following categories of active learning, and provides a number of examples:

- Cooperative Learning
- Writing to Learn
- Discovery Learning

Cooperative Learning

Cooperative learning requires more structure than simply having students work in pairs or small groups. This method holds students responsible for contributing to the learning of the entire group, while they also take responsibility for their own individual learning. Some teachers prefer to form these groups at the beginning of the course to maintain stability throughout the course; others form groups of shorter duration, as needed for particular activities.

When you set up cooperative learning groups, be sure to consider the following factors:

- What size group is optimal for the purpose you have in mind?
- Which students might work together most effectively?
- How will you assess student learning, both the group's as a whole and the individuals' within the group?

If you plan to use the same group throughout the course, you might want to wait until you have a sense of the students' abilities and personalities before forming the groups. While it is possible to group students early in the course before you know the dynamics, if you can balance the students in each group based on their strengths and weaknesses, the groups function better. If you are forming the groups on an *ad hoc* basis once the course is underway, it is easy to select group sizes and members based on your needs of the moment. We find it easier to assess student learning when the group functions for a longer period of time, because there are more assessment opportunities. However, the example of a short-term cooperative learning activity shown in Figure 5–2 illustrates how informal assessment can be accomplished even in a learning situation that can take less than half an hour.

This exercise engages students more immediately during a class session on the social and ethical issues related to information than does a lecture on the topic. It also serves to motivate students about these very interesting and important issues. The exercise meets a number of goals:

- It promotes active learning.
- It requires student cooperation within groups.
- It requires students to take ownership of the day's topics.
- It requires students to use knowledge and practice skills gained during the course.
- It challenges students to integrate newly gained knowledge with existing knowledge and to create a meaningful report.
- It promotes student confidence and satisfaction.
- It allows the instructor to informally assess students' searching behaviors and to re-emphasize important sources or techniques as needed.

**Exercise Example: Cooperative Learning for
Social and Ethical Uses of Information**

Description
This exercise is designed to be used near the end of an information literacy course, because it requires students to have good searching skills. Students work in groups to do research on topics related to the social and ethical uses of information, such as plagiarism, digital divide, and privacy or security on the Internet. Do not lecture on these topics during this class meeting, rather, ask the students to learn about these areas and to present what they have learned to the rest of the class in short, 2–4 minute, group presentations.

Preparation
At the end of the previous class, set up the activity as follows:
- Distribute fairly short articles to the students (newspaper articles work well) on the topics you have selected. Give a copy of the same article to each student in the group. Each student receives only one article, on his or her group's topic.
- Ask students to read the article as homework, and to bring the article to the next class.

Implementation
During the class in which you use this cooperative learning exercise, work through these tasks:
- Group students according to the article that they read. Each group must:

1. decide on the major theme or point of the article,
2. do additional research, using techniques they have learned during the course, and
3. get enough information to make a short presentation to the class about their topic.
- Assign students to a specific role within their group, based upon your knowledge of their personalities and abilities. These roles include:
  1. search moderator—to keep the searching on track,
  2. information manager—responsible for making sure that the information found is shaped into a cohesive presentation, and
  3. timekeeper/facilitator—helps to resolve group conflict, as well as watching the time.

Note: If you would like to use groups of four students, appoint both Web and database search moderators.
- Limit group time to 15–20 minutes. In that time, they must:
  1. select the key theme/topic,
  2. do their research, and
  3. shape a presentation.
- Give each group a handout that explains precisely what they need to do, and also lists each person's role (see Figure 6–3). Have them check the key theme they have identified with you before starting their research.
- Circulate amongst the groups during the working period, to make sure they are all on track, and that each participant is playing his or her assigned role.
- Let each group decide who will make the presentation.

Usually this activity can be completed in approximately half an hour, depending on the number of groups you have. However, if you have more time available, students can spend more time researching and shaping their presentations. This activity bolsters students' confidence in their searching abilities, and also provides a great deal of satisfaction at having met the time deadline, as well as having presented a cohesive report. The groups have a great deal of autonomy as they work, a motivating factor that we will touch on in Chapter 7.

Figure 5–2 Exercise Example: Cooperative Learning for Social and Ethical Uses of Information

If you have asked students to work in small groups throughout the course, they will feel at ease with the technique at this point. This activity, however, takes the process one step further, in that the students must be effective in their own roles for the entire group to succeed. The students should know one another well enough that they do not waste time becoming comfortable with each other, and those who present the reports will not be shy about doing so. It helps that each group has the power to decide who will present, or if all members of the group will share in presenting. Students also will have had most of the course to get used to their instructor's insistence that they themselves are responsible for their own learning. The handout listing students' roles and the precise assignment, shown in Figure 5–3, is very useful for answering questions students have about the oral directions.

Group Research Assignment

Based on newspaper article

Each person in your group has read the same article related to information in society.

As a group, I would like you to explore the topic of your article further, and then present a short report on the issue to the rest of the class.

You will need to:

1. Decide on the focus of the article, so you are agreed on the topic you will be researching further.
2. Allocate your time so that you can look for additional materials and synthesize what you have found in a short report.
3. Use your research skills to find additional material on this topic. This might include background information, items that elucidate a particular point, or information that updates what you found in your article.
4. Synthesize your findings. You may decide to have each person present a portion of your report, or appoint a reporter. However, I expect any group member to be able to answer questions based on the information you have found.

Time: 15 minutes for this group work before the reports start. Reports can last from 2–4 minutes.

Roles:

While each of you will participate in all 4 steps above, you also each have a specialized role.

Search Moderator:

Your job is to make sure that the searching is effective and that you find useful information.

Information Manager:

Your special role is to moderate the synthesis of the information, to make sure the group has what it needs and is shaping it into a coherent report.

Timekeeper and Facilitator:

Your job is to make sure the group work progresses in a timely fashion. You will also help resolve any group conflicts, and make sure the group selects a reporter or reporters.

Figure 5–3 Cooperative Learning Group Research Assignment

This particular cooperative learning activity probably would not work as well earlier in the course. Leaving aside the fact that their knowledge of searching and databases would be less well developed, students would be less likely to get right down to work in their groups, they would feel less comfortable presenting in front of the others, and they would be more likely to feel anxious, rather than confident about the short time allotted for the activity. Other types of cooperative learning activities would be more successful earlier, particularly ones that allow individuals more time to cohere as a group. Students who are less used to working in groups may need more time to become used to this technique.

Cooperative learning groups that last throughout the course may have more sophisticated methods of assessing student and group learning than in this example. In this case, the instructor is able to gauge the participation level of group members as she listens in on groups during their work session. The work of the group itself is evident during its presentation. Did they use appropriate sources? Did they use effective searching techniques to gather information? Were they able to use and communicate effectively the information that they found?

Numerous resources are available on cooperative learning. A particularly succinct and practical one is the chapter in Linda B. Nilson's book, *Teaching at Its Best* (Nilson, 1998). There, she describes the following important components of cooperative learning:

- Positive interdependence: students must feel responsible for the success of the group, and the success of each individual must depend in part on the group's success.
- Individual accountability: all group members are held responsible for their own learning and for the learning of other group members.
- Appropriate group composition, size and duration: heterogeneous groups in terms of ability, race, gender, and other characteristics help students to learn better, and also help to develop social skills.
- Face-to-face interaction: allow class time for group meetings.
- Genuine learning and challenge: students must learn, not just do, something.
- Explicit attention to collaborative social skills: the process is as important as the outcome (Nilson, 1998: 111–114).

Cooperative learning is a flexible teaching method that any teacher can effectively adapt in a variety of circumstances. The duration of a cooperative learning exercise may vary based on your goals and the length of the course; yet, a well-designed activity will engage students in ways beyond that of a simple active learning exercise. Plan carefully, based on Nilson's components, to maximize the benefit to students who participate in cooperative learning situations.

Writing to Learn

Writing to learn activities are another way to encourage students to take an active, rather than a passive, approach to learning. Because of their flexibility, you can use these activities both inside and outside of class, at the beginning, middle, or end of the class session. They have obvious benefits out of proportion to the small amount of time many of them take. They encourage students to focus on the subject at hand. Because students need to put something on paper, they reflect upon the material and have to organize their thoughts.

While the writing activity in Figure 5-4 is fairly basic — students only need to list items and explain them — they need to read more actively in order to pick out the major points, and to think about what the author means by them. Because they receive a grade for what they produce, more students will do the assignment than would do the reading alone.

> **Figure 5-4 Instructor Tip: Writing Assignment for Course Reading**
>
> Students, unfortunately, tend to neglect reading assignments. However, because these readings contain important material that supplements what you teach in the classroom, it is important to ensure that students read the materials more carefully (or read them at all). One way to accomplish this is to ask students to do a brief writing assignment based on a reading. They must list three major points of the material, with a brief explanation of each point. Such a writing assignment might count for several points in the course grade.

It is gratifying to watch students find the key points. The accompanying explanations frequently show real insight into the topics selected by the students. Students sometimes even relate the points to their own experience, often with enthusiasm.

You ask students to do this particular writing activity outside the classroom to enhance learning. Examples of in-class activities that you can assign to students might include:

- Create a list of what students would like to learn, given the topics of the day.
- Reflect on the relevance of a particular topic to each individual student.

- Write a paragraph on what the student recalls about the material covered in class that day.
- Identify one or two questions that students still have about a topic at the end of the session.
- Discuss the most important concept of the session.

Many, but not all, writing to learn activities reduce pressure on students by not requiring them to write polished pieces, or to put their names on their papers. These activities are often labeled free writing. Students spend just a few minutes putting their thoughts on paper without worrying about spelling and grammar. In some cases, the instructor may not even collect the sheets. Adding writing to learn activities is an easy way to begin engaging students more directly.

Instructors should use writing to learn activities with which they feel comfortable. For example, asking students to list what they would like to learn, given the topics of the day, might require an instructor to change the day's lesson plan on the spot. If an instructor is not comfortable with doing this, other writing to learn activities would be more suitable.

Beyond the short free writing ideas given above, see the two additional examples of writing to learn activities in Figures 5–5 and 5–6. One is an outside class assignment, the other is done in small groups in class.

Assignment Example: Information Seeking Behavior

This writing assignment can be given at the end of the first day of class. It is designed to have students reflect upon how they find information, and to compare their information seeking behaviors with those of another person. Students often notice that that either they or the person they interview tend to go to one type of source over and over again, at the same time realizing that other options exist. A project at the end of the course can be designed to encourage students to return to this early document, and realize how much their options have expanded.

Assignment:
Type one page (double-spaced) in which you define your own information-seeking behavior. Survey one other person on his/her information-seeking behavior and type one page about how they find and use information.

Figure 5–5 Assignment Example: Information Seeking Behavior (Adapted from Young and Harmony, 1999: 62.)

Exercise Example: Concept Maps

Use this activity during class time. It helps students make connections between the various topics included in the course. Students sometimes see each topic as isolated from other topics, rather than as forming a coherent whole.

- Arrange students in small groups.
- Supply them with a list of topics that you have covered in class to this point.
- Ask each group to draw a concept map using these topics.

While individuals usually engage in concept mapping by themselves, since each person makes his or her own connections between ideas, there are advantages to having students collaborate on this project. Students have different ideas about how to link topics, and their discussions, as they resolve these distinct notions, encourage further reflection upon the topics. In addition, students have varying levels of recollection about the different topics, and pooling their knowledge enables the activity to go more quickly.

**Figure 5–6 Exercise Example: Concept Maps
(Adapted from Weimer, 2002: 4–5.)**

The concept map assignment allows you to assess student learning and understanding, which is a feature of many writing to learn and free writing activities. See Chapter 7, Authentic Assessment, for more information about using concept maps for assessment. While the form of assessment may not be formal (particularly if students do not put their names on their papers), it helps instructors gauge the level of learning among students, and points out areas that might need review or further explanation.

Other writing to learn formats include logs and journals. These longer-term efforts may be directed in a number of ways, including asking students to write down reactions to course work, or to make connections between course work and the larger world. The instructor should provide explicit guidelines, and should review the journals or logs periodically, so that students feel that what they are doing is important. Such activities need not last throughout a course. The example in Figure 5–7 is an assignment that requires students to keep a log over a one-week period.

Assignment Example: Information Log

Keep an information need log for the coming week: each day, write down any instances when you needed information, and where you looked to get the information. This assignment can be neatly handwritten.

Figure 5–7 Assignment Example: Information Log

Students are often surprised to find out how often they look for information during a typical day. They tend to equate finding information to "finding information for a class paper or project." But through this assignment, they realize they are looking for information all the time: a ski report, the phone number of the pizza parlor, last night's ballgame score, or when a movie is playing. After completing this assignment, students tend to think about information very differently. It also seems to make them more receptive to what you are discussing in the course.

Writing to learn activities score particularly high on Keller's attention and relevance categories. Asking students to write is an effective attention-getting strategy. Writing during class is not a common activity (other than during exams). It also serves as a vehicle for relevance. Often you ask students to jot down what they think about the material or what they would like or still need to learn. Students appreciate being asked for their opinion or preferences.

Browse through the annotated Further Reading section at the end of this chapter. It provides a list of resources for additional ideas on writing to learn activities.

Discovery Learning

Discovery learning allows students to explore a topic before they formally learn it, or to expand upon what they do learn in class through additional exploration of their own. Discovery learning engages student attention. "Students find nothing so satisfying and intrinsically motivating as reasoning through a problem and discovering the underlying principle on their own" (Nilson, 1998: 58). Figure 5–8 highlights three attributes of discovery learning.

Attributes of Discovery Learning
• The creation, integration and generalization of knowledge through exploration and problem solving
• A process of learning driven by interest-based activities, in which the learner exercises some control over the sequence and frequency with which they occur
• Activities which strive to integrate new knowledge with the learner's existing knowledge base

**Figure 5–8 Attributes of Discovery Learning
(Bicknell-Holmes and Hoffman, 2000: 314)**

If you incorporate discovery learning activities in your classes, it is important to make them relevant to important course material. In addition, everyone benefits if the activities also relate to student interests.

Discovery learning activities can take place both within class and as assignments outside of class. If you plan to ask students to undertake a particularly challenging discovery exercise, you might want to organize it so that it will take place during the class session; that allows you to be available if students need assistance.

An example that takes place outside of class involves student comparison of an academic and public library. The assignment shown in Figure 5-9 is a very effective way to allow students to find out for themselves the differences between the two types of libraries. Talking about the topic in class is not as vivid or potent an experience.

Discovery Learning Homework Assignment

Name _____

What's in a name? A library is a library...or is it?

For this assignment you are required physically to visit two (2) different libraries. One of these must be a public library (see attached list of area public libraries with addresses and telephone numbers).
The other must be an academic library. We recommend the University at Albany's University Libraries; however, if you must use another academic library, please check with your instructor before doing so.

Your annotated bibliography topic_____
Answer the following questions.
ACADEMIC LIBRARY:
1. On what floor of the library is the reference desk located?

2. Locate an online public access catalog (OPAC). Examine the OPAC's initial search screen. Is there more than one way to search for material by subject? Yes_____ No_____
What are these search options called?

3. Using the EXACT SUBJECT option, enter into the catalog the topic that you have selected to use for the final bibliography project. Did you get any results?_____ How many?_____
4. Using the SUBJECT KEYWORD option, enter into the catalog the topic that you have selected to use for the final bibliography project. Did you get any results?_____. How many? _____.

Figure 5–9 Discovery Learning Homework Assignment (developed by Deborah Bernnard, University at Albany)

5. Locate a reference librarian. Ask the librarian to help you generate a list of alternate terms for your topic to enter into the catalog.
What are some of the terms you entered?
Did this strategy help you to retrieve better results?_____.
6. Locate two of the books from the catalog records that you have retrieved.
Record the following information for each of the books.
Book #1
Author   _____
Title   _____
Call #   _____
Publisher   _____
Date of Publication_____
Book #2
Author   _____
Title   _____
Call#   _____
Publisher   _____
Date of Publication_____
7. Now locate the periodicals section of the library. Periodicals include magazines, journals, and newspapers.
Browse the shelves and record 4 titles of journals and/or magazines that cover one (1) of the following broad subject areas (circle the subject area you select):
BUSINESS
EDUCATION
PSYCHOLOGY
SCIENCE
TECHNOLOGY
Journal or Magazine Titles:

1._____

2._____

3._____

4._____
Pay attention to the style of each journal or magazine. Try to determine if it is a scholarly publication or a popular publication. Overall, did you find more scholarly journals than popular journals in the academic library or did you find more popular than scholarly?

9. Record the citation for an article from one of the above journals or magazines, which is a primary source of information:
Author: _____
Title of Article:_____

Figure 5-9 continued

Title of Journal or Magazine: _____

Vol. # _____ Issue # _____ Date of publication_____

Page(s) of article_____

10. In your opinion, why is this a primary source?

PUBLIC LIBRARY:

1. What is the name of the library?

2. On what floor of the library is the reference desk located?

3. Locate an online public access catalog (OPAC). Examine the OPAC's initial search screen. Is there a choice of ways in which to search for materials on a topic? Yes_____ No_____

What are these search options called?

4. Using the SUBJECT option, enter into the catalog the topic that you have selected to use for the final bibliography project. Did you get any results?_____ How many?_____

5. Using the SUBJECT KEYWORD option, enter into the catalog the topic that you have selected to use for the final bibliography project. Did you get any results?_____How many?_____

6. Locate a reference librarian. Ask the librarian to help you generate a list of alternate terms that describe your topic to enter into the catalog. What are some of the terms you entered?

Did this strategy help you retrieve better results?

7. Locate 2 of the books from the catalog records that you have retrieved.

Record the author, title and call # for each of these books.

Book #1

Author _____

Title   _____

Call #   _____

Book #2

Author _____

Title   _____

Call #   _____

8. Now locate the periodicals section of the library. Periodicals include magazines, journals, and newspapers. Browse the shelves and record 4 titles of journals and/or magazines that cover one (1) of the following broad subject areas (circle the subject area you select):

BUSINESS

EDUCATION

PSYCHOLOGY

SCIENCE

TECHNOLOGY

Figure 5-9 continued

Journal or Magazine Titles:

1._____

2._____

3._____

4._____
Pay attention to the style of each journal or magazine. Try to determine if it is a scholarly publication or a popular publication. Overall, did you find more scholarly journals than popular journals in the public library or did you find more popular than scholarly?

9. Record the citation for an article from one of the above journals or magazines that is a secondary source of information:
Author: _____
Title of Article: _____
Title of Journal or Magazine:_____
Vol. # _____ Issue # _____ Date of publication_____
Page(s) of article_____

Figure 5-9 continued

An in-class exercise asks students to complete a worksheet exploring a general and a subject-specific database (Figure 5–10). The questions on the worksheet are fairly simple, so that students can complete it before you teach database structure or searching, even though this may be the first time some students will have encountered a bibliographic database. The questions are designed so that students will discover for themselves some key aspects of databases. The questions call on any knowledge students already have about searching, but also add to that knowledge. Students frequently have questions about the worksheet, which makes it most appropriate for use as an in-class exercise. This also helps so that you can advise individual students, after they finish the first side of the sheet, on the process of identifying an appropriate subject database. It is possible to assign topics for students to search, but, in the interest of student motivation, you might ask students to choose their own topics, perhaps related to other work they are doing in this or others courses. Suggesting that students use their own topics increases the relevance of the exercise, and therefore increases the motivation, as well. You could use this exercise just prior to a complementary assignment, in which students find scholarly and popular articles. They will appreciate the opportunity to get some of their searching done during class time.

In-Class Discovery Learning Exercise

Name _____

ELECTRONIC DATABASES ASSIGNMENT
You will be using the "Databases & E-Texts" link on the University
Libraries' Web Site:
http://library.albany.edu
Search your chosen annotated bibliography topic in EBSCO (*EBSCO
Academic Search Premier*). Answers to the first 3 questions will be found
in the "About" file for EBSCO (on the library's page, before you enter the
database itself).

ASSIGNMENT, PART ONE:

****Topic searched_____****

EBSCO
1. **What** years does this database/index cover?
2. **Does** the database have "full text" (complete articles)?
3. **Does** the database list more than journal or magazine articles;
   does it also include books, documents, other materials?
4. **Number of** "hits" or matches?
5. **Look at** first 10 "hits"—**how many** are relevant to what you're
   seeking?
6. **Did you** revise your search strategy? That is, did you do another
   search using different words?
7. **Did you** use the database thesaurus or index?

ASSIGNMENT, PART TWO:
Go to the "Databases & E-Texts" section of the Libraries' Web page.
Click on the subject most appropriate for your topic, and click on
"Indexes/Databases" in the right-hand box. Check the "About" screens
for each index. Pick the database that sounds most focused on your topic
area. Check it with your instructor before searching your selected topic in
this second database.
Name of the Database you have selected:_____

1. What years does this database/index cover?

2. Does the database have "full text" (complete articles)?

3. Does the database list more than journal or magazine articles?
   Does it also include books, documents, other materials?

4. Number of "hits" or matches?

5. Look at first 10 "hits"—how many are relevant to what you're
   seeking?

6. Did you revise your search strategy? That is, did you do another search using different words?

7. Did you use the database thesaurus or index?

8. Do the University Libraries own any of the articles/journals or magazines with the articles?

Figure 5–10 In-Class Discovery Learning Exercise (adapted from an exercise developed by Carol Anne Germain and Carol Anderson, University at Albany)

Of the three attributes of discovery learning listed in Figure 5–8, it is not difficult to meet the first:

• the creation, integration, and generalization of knowledge through exploration and problem solving,

or the third,

• activities which strive to integrate new knowledge with the learner's existing knowledge base.

However, it is more difficult to incorporate the second attribute,

• a process of learning driven by interest-based activities, in which the learner exercises some control over the sequence and frequency with which they occur.

Usually instructors have in mind certain activities that they would like all students to complete, and instructors generally have determined a logical order in which students should complete them. Chapter 6 explores the importance of autonomy for motivating students. It is possible to build in student control over discovery learning activities, while you address issues of autonomy. You might decide to offer several extra-credit discovery learning assignments. Students can opt to do these assignments or not, and if they decide to do them, they have control over when they complete them. You might also offer alternative assignments that meet the same goals, and allow students to select, buffet style, from the available options. Or, you might ask students to complete three out of five assignments during the course, allowing them to select the three they feel best meet their learning needs.

Bicknell-Holmes and Hoffman have explored the use of discovery learning specifically within the context of library instruction (2000).

They list five different categories of discovery learning structures (2000: 315–319):

- Case-based learning: students learn vicariously through stories or vignettes that illustrate the effective application of knowledge, skills, or principles. Students attempt to make decisions based on what they know about the content area.
- Incidental learning: students master concepts and ideas through an active learning strategy in which curricular content is linked to fun, game-like activities.
- Learning by exploring: also known as learning by conversing, student answers to questions about a particular topic or skill generate the learning.
- Learning by reflection: individuals learn to apply higher-level cognitive skills by modeling the interrogative patterns demonstrated by the instructor.
- Simulation based learning: students experience a learning opportunity in an artificial environment for developing and practicing a complex set of skills.

This study also provides two or three examples of activities for each category of discovery learning. Besides the examples in Figures 5-9 and 5-10, the Internet filtering example in Figure 3-3 qualifies as discovery learning (case-based), as does the cooperative group project on social and ethical aspects of information described earlier in Figure 5-2 (simulation-based).

Discovery learning techniques are most effective when the instructor can intersperse them with other teaching methods. As with all active learning techniques, it will take preparation time to develop activities that meet your goals, as well as the attributes for discovery learning. Logically, it is best to plan these activities when you initially design the course, to allow you time to reflect on your ideas, show them to others, perhaps even test them out on students serving as guinea pigs. But, should you have a sudden brainstorm for something new once the course starts meeting, by all means, try it out. Whether your discovery learning activity is long-planned or developed once the course is underway, keep a record of how it works, so that you will have this information when you start to revise the course in preparation for teaching it again.

Like other methods of actively engaging students, well-designed and integrated discovery learning methods have the potential to address all four of Keller's components of motivation: attention, relevance, confidence, and satisfaction. They also can prove extremely satisfactory to the instructor—it is exciting to see students work through exercises and problems, gaining and integrating skills and knowledge, and then using that knowledge and those skills in ways that anticipate future, real-world uses.

Key Characteristics of Active Learning Techniques

The chart in Figure 5–11 provides a quick overview of the key characteristics and strengths of each of the active learning techniques con-

> For example, in the cooperative exercise focusing on social and ethical issues concerning information (Figure 5–2), the instructor initially did not use the assignment sheet. Student confusion alerted her to the fact that they needed written instructions.

sidered in this chapter. Each type of activity has its place in an information literacy course, but it is important to match the appropriate technique with your instructional goals. Do not be afraid to experiment. Each activity that you try will stimulate ideas for revisions to increase the activity's effectiveness.

	Cooperative to Learn	Writing to Learn	Discovery Learning
Planning Needed	Extensive	Less extensive	Moderate
Who?	Pairs/groups	Individuals, usually	Frequently pairs or individuals
Duration	Short or long term	Frequently short term	Usually short term
Strengths	Social context of learning Ability to discuss and hear other opinions Shift in focus from instructor to students	Critical reflection Increases relevance for students Quick assessment method	Student exploration of topic Chance to integrate new knowledge with existing knowledge

Figure 5–11 Comparison of Active Learning Techniques

Before long, you will have a selection of proven techniques to use. But once you do, do not give up the excitement of trying new methods. Excellent ways to increase your repertoire include borrowing from colleagues and using tested methods included in some of the books and articles included in the resource list below.

ARCS Motivation Model and Actively Engaging Students

As has been highlighted throughout this chapter, active learning techniques, both in the classroom and through exercises and assignments, are effective motivators as measured against Keller's ARCS Model. Cooperative learning, writing to learn, and discovery learning effectively gain students' interest and attention. Professors in some of their other courses may not use these techniques, and they appreciate being able to take a more active role in their learning. You can design the actual content of the material taught through these methods to make it relevant to students. When you enable students to try something out, either on their own or with fellow students, the concepts of confidence and satisfaction come into play. Students learn by doing or through active cogitation and written expression. They can determine what they will do, and feel pride in their accomplishments. Instructors must carefully develop exercises, assignments, and other hands-on work to allow students to succeed, in order to bolster confidence and satisfaction. Whether in course-related instruction, or in information literacy courses, you can apply this principle.

Further Resources

Bicknell-Holmes, Tracy, and Paul Seth Hoffman. 2000. Elicit, Engage, Experience, Explore: Discovery Learning in Library Instruction. *Reference Services Review* 28, no. 4: 313–322. This article provides more information about discovery learning, and provides a host of ideas for using discovery learning in information literacy sessions and courses.

Fister, Barbara. 1990. Teaching Research as a Social Act: Collaborative Learning and the Library. *RQ* 29, no. 4 (Summer): 505–509. Fister emphasizes that collaborative learning provides a venue for teaching students about the social construction of knowledge, which may change their view of the library from a collection of tools and resources to a network of knowledge that the user joins. The author provides a few examples of teaching techniques, but the strength of this article is more theoretical than practical.

Gradowski, Gail, Loanne Snavely, and Paula Dempsey, eds. 1998. *Designs for Active*

Learning. Chicago: Association for College and Research Libraries. Chapters provide step-by-step instructions, exercises, and other materials for a variety of active learning sessions to use in the classroom. The book is divided into five sections: Basic Library Instruction, Searching Indexes and Online Catalogs, Search Strategies for the Research Process, Evaluation of Library Resources, and Discipline-Oriented Instruction.

Jacobson, Trudi E., and Timothy H. Gatti, eds. 2001. *Teaching Information Literacy Concepts: Activities and Frameworks from the Field*. Pittsburgh, PA: Library Instruction Publications. This book includes dozens of active learning activities grouped under the following categories: Course Frameworks and Assessment; Library and Research Skills and Strategies; Hierarchy of Learning, Publication Flow, and Formats; OPACs, Databases, and Indexes: Content and Searching; Internet Content and Evaluation; and Social, Ethical, and Legal Issues Related to Information.

Macklin, Alexius Smith. 2001. Integrating Information Literacy Using Problem-Based Learning. *Reference Services Review 29*, no. 4: 305–313. Macklin explains and provides examples of problem-based learning, a method of collaborative learning in which librarians and content area faculty can seamlessly integrate information retrieval directly into the curriculum. Problem-based learning falls into the category of simulation-based learning in the terminology used by Bicknell-Holmes and Hoffman.

Nilson, Linda B. 1998. *Teaching at Its Best: A Research Based Resource for College Instructors*. Bolton, MA: Anker Publishing. Chapter 13 is entitled "An Introduction to Student-Active Teaching: The Discovery Method," Chapter 18 is "Cooperative Learning," and Chapter 20 is "Writing-to-Learn: Activities and Assignments." Many additional chapters relate to the active engagement of students, as well.

Osif, Bonnie. 1999. Concept Mapping for Undergraduates. (December 2003) Available: www.library.northwestern.edu/transportation/slatran/bonnie.html.

Washington Center for Improving the Quality of Undergraduate Education. 1993. Collaborative Learning: 'Hearing Many Voices—Learning as One.' Special issue,*Washington Center News* 7, no. 3 (Spring). The "What is Collaborative Learning" article defines collaborative learning and describes a variety of different collaborative learning approaches. It also includes a valuable list of references. Available: www.evergreen.edu/washcenter/spring1993.htm.

References

Benware, Carl A., and Edward L. Deci. 1984. Quality of Learning with an Active Versus Passive Motivational Set. *American Educational Research Journal* 21, no. 4 (Winter): 755–765.

Bicknell-Holmes, Tracy, and Paul Seth Hoffman. 2000. Elicit, Engage, Experience, Explore: Discovery Learning in Library Instruction. Reference Services Review 28, no. 4: 313–322.

Karabenick, Stuart A., and Jan Collins-Eaglin. 1997. Relation of Perceived Instructional Goals and Incentives to College Students' Use of Learning Strategies. *The Journal of Experimental Education* 65, no. 4 (Summer): 331–341.

Lowman, Joseph. 1995. *Mastering the Techniques of Teaching*. 2nd ed. San Francisco: Jossey-Bass.

Nilson, Linda B. 1998. *Teaching at Its Best: A Research Based Resource for College Instructors*. Bolton, MA: Anker Publishing.

Weimer, Maryellen. 2002. Expand Use of Concept Maps to Encourage Conceptual Thinking. *The Teaching Professor* 16, no. 6 (June/July): 4–5.

Young, Rosemary M., and Stephena Harmony. 1999. *Working with Faculty to Design Undergraduate Information Literacy Programs*. New York: Neal-Schuman.

Chapter 6
Student Autonomy

Students who have the opportunity to make their own decisions regarding coursework are said to be more active, independent learners. It is possible to feel threatened when you first read about student autonomy being a motivator. How can you turn control of your course over to your students and still accomplish what you need to do? Won't they just vote not to hold class? Or spend their time surfing the Web if they did come to class? "No," your initial reaction might be, "I just can't do this."

But step back and think about examples of autonomy from your own life.

Do you feel the same way about the dreaded committee meeting you are forced to attend, as you do about the team meeting you helped to plan? Are you as excited about going to the football game (substitute opera, ballet, rock concert, company picnic, or other event as appropriate) that your friend or spouse feels you *must* attend, as the event you yourself chose to go to? Of course not (unless perhaps you are a saint). Now put yourself in the place of your students, and consider what autonomy they have in your class.

Student Choices

Students can decide to come to class or not. They can participate during class if they so choose. They can do their homework, or not. In some cases, they can select their own topics for class projects or class assignments. The authors require an annotated bibliography as a final project, and students are able to choose a topic of interest—either something they are studying or writing about in another course, or a personal interest or hobby.

Letting students select their own topic really is not momentous. Students interested in their topic will be more interested in working on their course project. In other words, interested students translate into motivated students. So maybe student autonomy without chaos is indeed possible.

Note the areas that students typically control, other than paper topics: attendance, participation, and homework completion. We can view each of these as a continuum from positive to negative. What might be positive for instructors (attendance, participation) might seem the opposite to a student, who has competing interests and demands on his or her time. Students are not motivated to attend courses that fall low in their hierarchy of important activities, nor are they willing to spend time working on homework and other projects for such courses. Throughout this book, we present a variety of ideas for increasing student motivation. This chapter considers the effect autonomy has on motivation, and offers suggestions for changing course components to increase student autonomy. We do not ask you to give up complete control of your classroom, only to motivate students by giving them some freedom.

Allowing students choices is even more important in a required course than it is in a course in a student's major, or in an elective course. Students often do not have an inherent interest in information literacy, as they might in one of these other types of courses. Instructors are often able to help stimulate student interest, but it takes more effort given the nature of the course. Giving students choices in the course, more choices than they might be offered in many of their other courses, will intrigue them, and will draw them into the selection process, and hence the course itself. Therefore, in this chapter we discuss the following issues related to student autonomy:

- ARCS Motivation Model and Student Autonomy
- Caveats
- Implementing Student Autonomy

ARCS Motivation Model and Student Autonomy

Granting students autonomy meets several of Keller's Motivation Model requirements. Depending on the amount of autonomy that you give to students, you may very well get their attention. Students often operate with little autonomy in their courses, so if you break the mold, they will sit up and take notice. In the process, you will also be making the course more relevant to them, since they will be able to make their own decisions in some aspects of the course. Keller states that allowing students to assume personal control is one way to build confidence.

> Most people seem to enjoy feeling that they have some control over their lives and environment. Yet, in a learning setting, the control is often clearly in the hands of an instructor. To enhance motivation, the controlling influence of the instructor should be focused in the areas of leading the experience, and adhering to the standards that are expected. This provides a stable learning environment in which the learner should be allowed as much personal control over the actual learning experience as possible. (Keller, 1987: 5)

However, only some students may feel more confident as they make their own decisions. The usual classroom mold, which infrequently gives students much choice, causes some students, at least initially, to resent having to make their own decisions in a more autonomous setting. These students may need extra support as they adjust to this new model. The last of Keller's four elements is "satisfaction with the process or results of the learning experience" (Keller, 1987: 2). Students who believe that they have a degree of control over some aspect of the course will tend to feel more satisfaction with the process than they would otherwise.

Caveats

With all of the ideas presented in this chapter, as with many of the ideas presented in this book, readers need to keep some things in mind.

- Consider your comfort level, and start building autonomy into your course gradually. Your changes will not be effective if you have bitten off more than you can, or would like to, chew. Your students will sense your lack of commitment, which will lead to difficulties. Also, you do not want to promote anarchy in your course!
- Consider your students' developmental level, and gauge what you think they will be able to handle. Students can perceive choices as threatening (consider those students who do not even want to choose their own paper topic); so do not overwhelm them.
- Consider asking students to make choices as part of a group, rather than by themselves. This will result in a more manageable number of possible changes, will provide students with a support group, and will facilitate discussion about the changes prior to their adoption. Something that initially sounds good might not be so great once students toss the idea around.

- Consider the impact your class size will have on some of the changes that you might entertain. Instructors can institute significant aspects of autonomy even in large classes, though others are easier with smaller classes.
- Consider that this partnership model of teaching does not have to be an equal partnership (Ramsey and Couch, 1994: 149). Do not feel shy in pointing this out to your students.

Implementing Student Autonomy

Let's take a look at the areas in which you might want to incorporate some student autonomy (see Figure 6–1), and the actual ways in which you might do this. The ideas proposed in the first two categories may feel the least threatening, as you think about giving students more autonomy.

AVENUES FOR STUDENT AUTONOMY
Course activity Course assignments Course policy Course content Student assessment
Figure 6–1 Avenues for Student Autonomy (Adapted from Weimer, 2001)

Course Activity

As the instructor, you generally decide how to conduct the course. Will you lecture? Use active learning techniques? Have in-class group or individual activities? Ask students to make presentations? You also decide which of these elements you will combine to fill the allotted class time, and which types of activities to pair with each slice of content. Obviously, you keep in mind student attention spans and learning styles when you make your decisions. Have you ever, though, consulted the students themselves about these issues? Or allowed them to make some decisions about the activities that will fill the class time?

You might ask students what their preferred learning styles are, and see if several styles predominate. If so, you might tell students that you will use methods that address these styles when feasible. Midway through the course, ask the students if these methods are working. Would they like you to try other teaching styles?

Another way to give students a choice in classroom activities comes with active learning exercises. You might develop two or three ways to meet a class objective. We describe an example in Figure 6-2.

Even something as minor as the length of a class break (when the class is long enough to warrant one) can be a vehicle for student choice.

Figure 6-2 Instructor Tip: Boolean Operator Learning Options

If you are teaching Boolean operators, you might let students select from these possibilities:

- Work through a Web-based tutorial.
- Read a chapter from their textbook on the topic.
- Work within a small group to teach themselves (provide a variety of resources).

Once students have completed one of the above, ask them individually or in groups to share their learning, by doing one of the following (you can select one or you might let them choose their preferred option):

- Review one Boolean operator's use with the rest of the class, providing examples and exercises.
- Write a short guide to Boolean operators (or one particular operator) for a novice.
- Complete an exercise sheet that you have developed to gauge learning.

One of the authors did not realize that the breaks she gave during a three-hour class were not up to student expectations. When she switched from 10 minute to 15 minute breaks, based on comments written on midcourse assessment forms, students spent less time worrying about the break and more time thinking about learning.

Course Assignments

This is the arena where instructors may find it easiest to arrange for student autonomy. You may already give your students choices, such as paper or presentation topic, or doing an additional assignment to earn extra credit.

Similar to the learning options in Figure 6-2, you might develop two or three assignments all of which meet the same objective, and allow students to select the one they prefer to do, as in Figure 6-3. In this case, it is important to make sure each assignment is at the same level. If you offer a selection that includes a particularly easy one and an identifiably difficult one, do not be surprised if the easy option is the option of choice (Weimer, 2001: 1).

A few years ago, one of the authors decided to add an element of choice to her information literacy course by allowing students either to give the standard final presentation for the course, or to replace teaching one small segment of the course for the presentation. The author and the student would meet to agree on the topic to be taught, to make sure that it was something that interested the student, and that it was not too complex. While several students every quarter complain about the five-minute final presentation, only one student has ever opted to teach a small segment of the course. The author would like to see this happen more, and will retain this choice in her syllabus. However, this highlights the importance of making the choices attractive to the students, while maintaining equal learning goals.

Assignment Example: Information Seeking Behavior

Information Seeking Behavior Assignment
I would like you to reflect upon how you go about finding information. You have a choice about how you may fulfill this assignment. Please select one of the following options and be prepared to submit your paper or to present your response to the class next week. All written assignments must be word processed.

- Read chapter 2, "The Business of Understanding," in Richard Wurman's book, Information Anxiety 2. Write one page on how the categories of data, information, knowledge and wisdom relate to your search for information. In addition, write one page relating the LATCH framework to the way you organize your information.
- Write one page on how you prefer to find information. Consider both information that you need on a day-to-day basis and information that you need for academic endeavors. Interview one other person (a friend, sibling, parent, professor) and write one page on their information seeking behaviors.
- Prepare a three-minute presentation to the class on how you find and organize information, both information that you need on a day-to-day basis and information that you need for academic reasons.
- Create a collage that represents the methods that you use to find information, both in your personal life and for academic needs. Be prepared to explain your collage to your classmates.

Figure 6–3 Assignment Example: Information Seeking Behavior

You might also have the class help you to determine assignment due dates (Weimer, 2001:1). If you are amenable to students submitting their assignments on a number of different dates, you can individualize the due dates. If this is not manageable, the date upon which you agree would apply to the entire class.

Your students might also help you to determine the weight you place on each paper, worksheet, or other project. If you have a number of assignments all worth the same number of points, you might allow students to opt out of one of the assignments, or to drop the grade for the lowest of these assignments. For more ideas on grading, see the section on Student Assessment later in this chapter.

Course Policy

If you reexamine your course syllabus, you may find several areas of course policy that you are willing to open up to student feedback. Often instructors clearly lay out their attendance policies. Are you willing to negotiate with students on the number of unexcused absences you will accept? Might a student make up an absence by successfully completing an online tutorial on the topic? Another area related to attendance is penalties for absences and possible rewards for coming to class. Perhaps the students might help you decide on these. Once they have a stake in decision making related to attendance, they may think twice about not coming to class.

Most courses have policies about assignment deadlines, after which the instructor will not accept assignments, or will reduce the grade. Students might help you determine how long you might accept assignments beyond the due date, and what should happen to the grades for these items.

If you give numerous quizzes in your course, you might allow the class as a whole the option of having all of them count, or offer to drop each person's lowest quiz grade. While it will not take much pondering to determine which option the average class will select, it does give students a sense of control.

You want to encourage students to participate actively in your course, but this can be a tough area to grade. For example, it is often difficult to determine if quiet students are

- daydreaming,
- processing course material,
- totally out of it, or
- shy.

You might let students determine what characterizes meaningful participation in the course and help set the course policy for participation (Weimer, 2001: 1).

Many instructors have policies governing classroom management. One such policy, found in the syllabus in Figure 3–5, requires students "to contribute to an environment conducive to the learning of all students." While you probably do not want to open up discussion on changes to a policy such as this one, you might ask students to determine what behaviors would accomplish this. Engaging students on this topic provides an opportunity to start building community, as well as emphasizing the importance of the policy. Another classroom management issue focuses on the timely arrival of students. If disruptions associated with students coming to class late concern you, you might want to discuss this issue openly with the class. Explain to them why you feel as you do, and ask them to put themselves in your place. Solicit their ideas about what would discourage such disruptions and encourage on time attendance.

> Due to numerous late stragglers who disrupt class, we have developed a policy that we shut the classroom door five minutes into the class, and late arrivals have to wait until the break before they can enter the classroom. While this policy is not one of the items over which we give our students a choice, it is usually very effective. However, it can sometimes take nerves of steel to refuse students admittance if they arrive just a few moments after the door is closed. If the instructor and the class members come to agreement on a way to deal with late arrivals, it might be easier to enforce it.

Course Content

In developing courses, instructors often would like to include more topics than sound pedagogical theory will endorse. As instructors, we winnow the topics that we would like to teach to a manageable number, but most likely lament those topics that we had to discard. One way to provide students with some autonomy regarding class content is to use those discarded, but still valuable, topics in a different capacity. Provide students with a list of all the topics that the course could cover. Ask them which ones they feel would be most useful to them. Maintain the right to include topics that you feel are critical, but also include some of those that the students feel most strongly about, even if they were originally on your discard list. Your willingness to include topics that are relevant to their needs and interests will significantly motivate students.

A less radical variation of this is to provide a list of the course topics, but to tell students that you will spend more time on those topics that they feel are most important or that they need the most help with. Ask them to work in small groups to identify these topics. Working with others will give each student a chance to discuss a topic, facilitating understanding of what is actually meant by the topic and allowing students to gauge what they actually do know, as they try to articulate ideas or compare their knowledge to that of their classmates.

You might also ask students, very early in the course, to write about what they hope to learn during the course, or what information literacy skills they feel will be important to know (Weimer, 2001: 2). You could then incorporate their input into your design of the course for that semester or quarter.

If you use these ideas, you will probably find that you cannot cover all the areas that students feel are important. A minority of students will place a different emphasis on certain topics than the majority of the students. You might still be able to use this student input. Ask students to take responsibility for learning certain topics, and then to teach those topics to the rest of the class. They might do this through a short presentation during the course, or you might incorporate it into the final course project. We ask our students to do five-minute presentations on the last day of class about their annotated bibliography topics and how researching them have affected their information literacy skills. We could change this assignment entirely, and ask all students to teach a new topic, not otherwise taught during the course, for five minutes during the class period previously set aside for final presentations. Since students learn best when they prepare to teach others, this tactic would allow you to introduce more topics into the class, enhance student learning on the part of those teaching, and show that we value topics that students feel are important.

If there is no time for students to share material that they feel is important, you might build an assignment into the course in which students write one or two individual learning objectives beyond the ones shared by the whole class. Require each student to share these learning objectives with you, and help them to develop a strategy for meeting their personalized objectives, along with a mechanism for assessing their learning (Ramsey and Couch, 1994: 151).

An easy way to connect student interests to class material is to use examples that are meaningful to them, as described in Chapter 4. At the start of the course, ask students about their interests and hobbies. Use some of these items later in the course when you need topics as examples, such as topics for database searching.

Student Assessment

Students feel differing levels of anxiety about the various elements of the course that instructors count toward their grades. Some students would prefer to do almost anything other than make a presentation, while others feel that the format of a test does not accurately convey their knowledge about a subject. One easy to implement idea that allows students to have some control over grading involves adding an optional assignment. While you could make this assignment worth extra credit points, it is possible to use it in another way to diminish student anxiety. Offer to count this optional assignment for a certain number of points, and tell students you will then reduce the points for another assignment by an equal amount. See Figure 6-4 for an example.

If you would like to offer extra credit assignments but have concerns about the extra work that might be involved, it will relieve you to know that many instructors find that only the better students in a class avail themselves of extra credit options. The small amount of additional grading required, therefore, is usually not a burden, and it allows diligent students the chance to be even more diligent, which they find reassuring.

Figure 6-4 Instructor Tip: Optional Assignment and Grading

To foster autonomy, give students some control over the percentage value of their projects. For example, in one course students are required to do a final presentation that incorporates everything they have learned in class. This presentation is worth 40% of the grade. However, those students who opt to write a short paper will have their paper count for 10% of their grade, and their presentation only 30%. This offers students who are shy of public speaking the opportunity to have more control over an area that makes them anxious. Generally fewer than one quarter of the students actually avail themselves of such opportunities, so it doesn't lead to a great deal of extra grading. Those who do decide to write the paper, however, welcome the option and the control that it gives them.

If you do not already offer students the choice of submitting drafts of larger assignments, or require them to, consider doing so. When students have a chance to review feedback on their work and then revise it, their opportunities for meaningful learning increase. You also give students an element of control, in that they are able to do better work and hence earn a better grade. Figure 6-5 describes one example of a project that builds in feedback throughout the process.

Another way to allow students some say in evaluation is to let them establish the criteria by which you grade them (Weimer, 2001: 2). This might hark back to decisions about the definition of meaningful participation and the number of absences allowed. It might also include what elements are important for an assignment, which

---

Figure 6-5 Instructor Tip: Feedback on Assignment Drafts

The final project for our information literacy course is a ten-item annotated bibliography on a topic of the student's choice. The items include such things as a book, a scholarly journal article, a popular magazine article, and primary and secondary sources. Each week, students submit their citations and annotations for two or three of these items. We provide feedback on both format and content, and they are able to revise the items for the final project. Hence, they have a great deal of control over their grade for this portion of the course.

---

assignments you will grade based on student choice, and how many points you will attach to each assignment. The article by Hiller and Hietapelto (2001) offers a detailed analysis of contract grading. They address various ways to implement contract grading, with examples from course syllabi. Upon polling their students, they found that an overwhelming majority preferred a contract to traditional grading, even if they had no previous experience with the model. You would likely limit the contract grading elements up for negotiation in a lower-level information literacy course compared to those in an upper level undergraduate course.

Students use a variety of methods to plot how well they are doing in their courses; but, one of these is the obvious one of how well they do on quizzes and exams. While information literacy courses, perhaps due to short duration, may not include a midterm or final exam, they may administer frequent quizzes. A key purpose of such quizzes is to make sure that students are taking the course, both content and attendance, seriously. However, an experienced professor has said that his students appreciate the sense of control that they feel about his frequent quizzes (Beidler and Beidler, 1993: 23–24). When he polled one of his classes, 61 out of 62 students felt that they learned more through daily quizzes than they would have done with the standard longer exams and final. Beidler explains why his students were enthusiastic about the quizzes: quizzes "encourage them to keep up with the reading in my course—which often makes it the *only* course they are caught up with. But more important, my quizzes ask questions only on the material assigned for that particular day, so students feel that they have some control over their academic fates" (Beidler and Beidler, 1993: 23–24).

Was it possible our information literacy students might feel the same way as did Beidler's students? We assumed that they probably hated the quizzes. It was time to poll them, just as Beidler did. One of the authors polled her students on their feelings about the weekly quizzes. Her findings closely paralleled Beidler's: the quizzes did not cause them much anxiety, and did motivate them to review course material before each class.

Final Thoughts on Student Autonomy

In this chapter we presented a number of ideas to consider if you would like to highlight student autonomy in your course. Are we advocating giving too much control to our students? We do not think so, based on the positive motivational effects that we have seen. Remember that you control the process of giving students autonomy. Think through exactly which area or areas are most comfortable for you to modify. Select one or two ways to start, based on your own sense of comfort and your feelings about how your students will react. Do not be shy about asking your students, partway through or at the end of the course, how these nontraditional elements of the course worked for them. As you grow into the changes you have made, and as you gather data about the effectiveness of these changes in motivating students, you may want to consider adding other elements that enhance student autonomy. Do not let nightmares of students running amok keep you from taking the first step. Consider your differing reactions to activities that you have selected compared to ones required of you. Students typically take four or five courses each semester. By enhancing student autonomy, your course will really stand out, and you will see the effects on your students' motivation levels.

References

Beidler, Peter G., and Gretchen M. Beidler. 1993. What's Your Horse: Motivating College Students. *Journal on Excellence in College Teaching* 4: 9–26.

Hiller, Tammy Bunn, and Amy B. Hietapelto. 2001. Contract Grading: Encouraging Commitment to the Learning Process Through Voice in the Evaluation Process. *Journal of Management Education* 25, no. 6 (December): 660–684.

Keller, John M. 1987. Strategies for Stimulating the Motivation to Learn. *Performance and Instruction* 26, no. 8 (October): 1–7.

Ramsey, V. Jean, and Peter D. Couch. 1994. Beyond Self-directed Learning: A Partnership Model of Teaching and Learning. *Journal of Management Education* 18, no. 2 (May): 139–161.

Weimer, Maryellen. 2001. Let Students Make Classroom Decisions. *Teaching Professor* 15, no. 1 (January): 1–2.

Chapter 7
Authentic Assessment

The assessment methods you use in the classroom can have a pronounced effect on student motivation. Consider the following potential characteristics of student assessment and grading:

- Lacks a clear explanation of grading criteria
- Lacks an opportunity for feedback before grade is assigned
- Asks only for recall of discrete pieces of knowledge
- Lacks a connection to what students will do in the real world
- Is based on a curve

Assessment tools that embody one or more of these characteristics are not unusual, but none of these items act as motivators. This chapter introduces a number of assessment ideas that help to motivate students. We also explain why projects and assignments with the characteristics above should be avoided.

What Is Authentic Assessment?

Traditional assessment generally means tests, quizzes, and papers. A course might include a midterm and a final, both of which are graded on a curve, two small papers that do not require research, and one long term paper that does require research. Authentic assessment methods for the same course would look very different. A similar course using authentic assessment might include some quizzes, a number of short writing projects, and solution of a case study. In addition, the directions for these assignments, their supporting material, and the grading scheme would be very different.

Montgomery describes what authentic assessment sets out to do:

> Students now are being asked to demonstrate, in a meaningful way, what they know and are able to do. Rather than measuring discrete, isolated skills, authentic assessment emphasizes the application and use of knowledge. Authentic assessment includes the holistic performance of meaningful, complex tasks in challenging environments that involve contextualized problems. Authentic tasks are often multidimensional and require higher levels of cognitive thinking such as problem solving and critical thinking. (Montgomery, 2002: 35)

In addition, authentic assessment is concerned not only with a product, but also with the process students go through to create that product (Montgomery, 2002: 35).

So let us compare our two hypothetical course assessment scenarios again (Figure 7–1).

Course Using Traditional Assessment	Course Using Authentic Assessment
Midterm and final Measures discrete skills or knowledge Only considers product Student's performance depends on class performance (grading on a curve)	Quizzes throughout the course Measures discrete skills or knowledge Focuses more on process, provides more opportunities to succeed Student's performance based entirely on his/her ability/knowledge
Short papers No clear criteria for grading No feedback before grade is given No real-life context	Short writing projects Rubric used for grading Drafts submitted for feedback Real-life connection aimed for
Extensive research paper No clear criteria for grading No feedback before grade No real-life context	Case study analysis Rubric used for grading Drafts submitted for feedback Real-life connection

Figure 7–1 Assessment Comparison

Related Assessment Terms

This section provides explanations of a number of other terms related to assessment that will be used in this chapter.

Formative Assessment

Formative assessment is an ongoing process directed toward improving student learning. Assignments that include the submission of drafts are a type of formative assessment. The feedback students receive on the drafts allows them to learn from their mistakes and to revise the work they have done. Formative assessment also provides useful feedback to you, as the instructor. If the feedback indicates that students are not learning what you think they ought to be, you can change the teaching methods you are using.

Summative Assessment

Summative assessment is a final assessment of a student's knowledge or skills. In this type of assessment, the feedback that students receive is not designed to promote additional learning, but to evaluate a finished product.

Alignment

When you design assessment techniques to use in your information literacy course, be careful that they align closely to other aspects of your instruction. A technique might be useful in the motivational sense, but be otherwise unrelated to what you hope to accomplish and what you expect the students to learn. For example, you might decide to implement peer assessment (students assessing their classmates). However, if you do not use the students' comments in determining grades, or you do not spend enough time teaching your students how to assess their peers, this method would not align with your goals for the course.

Cognitive Assessment and Performance Assessment

As you explore authentic assessment further, you may run into two related terms: cognitive assessment and performance assessment. Reeves defines cognitive assessment as "focused on measuring students' higher order thinking abilities, attitudes, and communication skills" (Reeves, 2000: 107). He defines performance assessment as "methods that require learners 'to demonstrate their capabilities directly, by creating some product or engaging in some activity.' Performance assessment is focused on learners' abilities to apply knowledge, skills, and judgment in ill-defined realistic contexts whereas traditional testing largely measures inert knowledge that can be cued by a few artificial stimuli" (Reeves, 2000: 107). Both cognitive and performance assessment fall within authentic assessment, and examples of each are included later in this chapter.

Classroom Assessment

Angelo and Cross write about classroom assessment in their highly influential book, *Classroom Assessment Techniques* (1993). Classroom assessment uses feedback from students to assess and improve one's own teaching as a way of improving student learning. "There are gaps, sometimes considerable ones, between what was taught and what has been learned....To avoid such unhappy surprises, faculty and students need better ways to monitor learning throughout the semester. Specifically, teachers need a continuous flow of accurate information on student learning" (Angelo and Cross, 1993: 3).

There are seven characteristics of classroom assessment, some of which relate to student motivation levels. Classroom assessment is centered on the learner, teacher-directed, mutually beneficial to both students and teacher, formative rather than summative, context-specific, and ongoing (Angelo and Cross, 1993: 4). By their very nature, classroom assessment tools are closely aligned to course content and goals. Frequently, they fall under the category of cognitive assessment. An example of a cognitive classroom assessment technique that is well-aligned to the rest of the course involves asking students to spend a few minutes at the end of class period answering two questions:

What is the main point I learned today?

What was the main point left unanswered in today's session?

(Biggs, 1999: 109)

Classroom assessment provides a framework for powerful, easily instituted tools to check student learning. Several classroom assessment tools are described later in this chapter.

Effective Assessment

Keep in mind that in order for assessment to be effective, you should use a variety of different methods, you should use them throughout your course, and they should be integrated into your goals and methods for the course. Consider these points when you reflect upon the assessment techniques you already use and when you read through the ideas for authentic assessment contained in this chapter. Are there additional techniques you might use productively? Are there other points in your course when assessment—perhaps informal, formative, classroom assessment—would be appropriate? And how well do your assessment methods align with other aspects of your course? If you are developing a new course, you should plan for assessment as part of the design process, in order to incorporate these effective assessment practices. For existing courses, retrofitting in accordance with these practices is fine.

ARCS Motivation Model and Authentic Assessment

Confidence

Key features of authentic assessment fit Keller's ARCS Motivation Model, particularly in regard to confidence and satisfaction. One component of confidence is personal control: "To enhance motivation, the controlling influence of the instructor should be focused in the areas of leading the experience, and adhering to the standards that are expected" (Keller, 1987: 5). This phrase was quoted in Chapter 6 in relationship to student autonomy. With assessment, the focus is on the latter part of the sentence, "adhering to the standards that are expected." If you provide students with the criteria by which they will be graded, they will feel a sense of control over the work that you expect of them. Consider that many instructors give very little description of what distinguishes an excellent paper or project from one that is good or poor. Students feel uncertain and may even feel that grading is at the whim of their instructor. If you give students a rubric, or set of criteria, by which their paper or project will be judged, they will understand much better what you are looking for, and will have an increased sense of control. You will find more information on rubrics later in the chapter, along with some examples of rubrics for information literacy courses.

You might find other ways to increase students' control over how well they do in the course. Forsyth and McMillan suggest methods such as holding workshops on study skills, time management, and effective reading; providing helpful resources such as class outlines, notes, additional readings, or question and answer sessions; and allowing students some say in what assessment procedures are used for the course (1991: 57). All of these methods can increase the confidence of those students who decide to take advantage of the opportunities.

Satisfaction

Keller posits three components of satisfaction: natural consequences, positive consequences, and equity (see Figure 7–2).

Components of Satisfaction	
Natural Consequences	One of the most rewarding results of performance-oriented instruction is to use the newly acquired skills or knowledge.
Positive Consequences	These are used to reinforce learners' successes. A combination of positive reinforcements and extrinsic rewards can be helpful.
Equity	Make performance requirements consistent with stated expectations, and provide consistent measurement standards.

**Figure 7–2 Components of Satisfaction
(Adapted from Keller, 1987: 5–6)**

Authentic assessment offers you the opportunity to fold all three components of satisfaction into your course.

Natural Consequences

Keller asserts, "One of the most rewarding results of performance-oriented instruction is to use the newly acquired skills or knowledge" (1987: 5). Traditional forms of assessment do not offer learners this reward. While it might be satisfying to be able to fill in the blanks or circle the right answer on a test, the satisfaction is not as profound as being able to actually do something one has learned, and do it well. Students who are able to successfully solve a real-world case study based upon what they have learned in a course will feel a great sense of satisfaction.

Positive Consequences

It is appropriate to use both intrinsic and extrinsic methods of motivation. "Even when people are intrinsically motivated to learn the material, there are likely to be benefits from extrinsic forms of recognition. For example, public acknowledgement of achievement, privileges, students presentations of products, and enthusiastically positive comments are generally welcome" (Keller, 1987: 6). Instructors might comment on the high quality of responses to classroom assessment methods or to group problem-solving or case study presentations. If students are involved in activities that are particularly relevant to them, or that mirror real-life situations with which they will be faced, positive recognition will be more meaningful to them than it would be in "drill and practice exercises" (Keller, 1987: 6).

However, be careful about the stress that you place on extrinsic motivators. Use quizzes and a variety of classroom assessment techniques as a way to provide feedback to students about how they are doing. "Instructors who stress tests, evaluations, and grades over all else, however, produce students who are striving to earn a particular grade rather than to learn the course material" (Forsyth and McMillan, 1991: 55).

Some instructors who use traditional methods of assessment use norm-referenced grading systems: they grade on a curve. Forsyth and McMillan warn against using this type of grading. "When instructors grade on a curve, they ensure that some students in the class will earn failing grades. This grading scheme reinforces negative expectations, promotes competition among students, and limits the number of students who receive positive reinforcement" (1991: 58).

Equity

You want students to feel good about how much they have accomplished, but frequently students compare themselves to others. "A student might achieve a new 'personal best,' a score that is higher than any he or she ever achieved before. But, if it is lower than someone else's with whom the student was making a personal comparison, satisfaction might still be low" (Keller, 1987: 6). Rubrics will guard against inconsistent and inequitable measurement standards. Other assessment tools, such as portfolios, will allow a student to see how far he or she has progressed during a course. Portfolios provide concrete evidence to a student about their personal accomplishments, leaving them less likely to decide to compare apples (their own progress) to oranges (another student's).

Types of Authentic Assessment

This section will take a look at five types of authentic assessment techniques:

- Rubrics
- Concept Mapping
- Minute Writing
- Cases
- Portfolios

Using a mix of assessment methods is desirable, and you might find some ideas you can use among these types. Keep in mind that it is not necessary to use all of them, and some methods might not work in certain situations. If you are teaching a course that only meets seven or ten times, it might be impossible to ask students to assemble a portfolio of their work. However, some of these methods are extremely flexible and take little or no class time. They may fit in very well even in an information literacy course of short duration.

Rubrics

Rubrics are clearly spelled out criteria that you use when grading an assignment. Rubrics are helpful for a number of reasons:

- They make grading easier for you
- They make grading more equitable
- They help students understand just what you are looking for
- They help students succeed on the assignment
- They help to motivate students by increasing student confidence
- They boost student motivation by increasing equity

If you have not developed a rubric before, there are a variety of models available to give you ideas. Rubrics are frequently used in schools, and these can be adapted if you are in a higher education setting (Schrock, 2002). There are also models for rubrics developed specifically for college students (Beck, 2001; Montgomery, 2002) and for Web-based lessons (Pickett and Dodge, 2001).

Before we started using a rubric for our annotated bibliography final project, we often despaired over some of the papers that were turned in. Why did so many students forget to alphabetize their entries? We clearly explained in the syllabus and in class that this was important. Why did they fail to label each entry with the source category? We spelled this out, too. We also reminded them on the weekly drafts. Weren't they reading the guidelines for the assignment? Our frustration was hitting the boiling point. We decided to use a rubric for this annotated bibliography project. We passed the rubric out in class at just about the midpoint of the course, when students were thinking more and more about the final project. We went over the rubric (as we had gone over the assignment guidelines in the syllabus some weeks before), and asked students to keep it at hand when they were working on this project. We do still see some bibliographies that aren't alphabetized or that lack source category labels, but they are fewer than in the past. In addition, fewer students complain that they do not know what is expected on the assignment, and fewer come back to complain after they see their final grade for this project.

All rubrics include features that:

- Focus on measuring a stated objective (performance, behavior, or quality)
- Use a range to rate performance
- Contain specific performance characteristics arranged in levels indicating the degree to which the standard has been met (Pickett and Dodge, 2001)

The rubric used to grade the authors' annotated bibliography provides an example of a rubric (Figure 7–3). This rubric, adapted from one developed by Beck (2001), is scored on a twenty-five-point system, since the assignment is worth 25 percent of the students' grades.

By using examples, it is not difficult to develop rubrics for your own course assignments. These assignments may range from the development of effective database or Internet search strategies, to critical evaluation of information resources, to analyzing and solving case studies related to the ethical use of information. Rubrics can successfully be developed for all these assignments. You just need to be clear on what it is you are measuring and what the range of performance is for each item of measurement, along with characteristics to identify where a student is on that range.

Annotated Bibliography Rubric			
Name_____ **FINAL PROJECT GRADE PROFILE** *Annotated Bibliography*			
Criteria	*Description*	*Level*	*Score*
Thesis Statement (1 point)	Lacks Thesis Statement	0 pts.	
	Thesis Statement present	1 pt.	
Correct Sources (10 pts.)	Fewer than ten categories, or items listed for categories do not match the category (1 point deduction for each mistake)	0–9 pts.	
	All ten source categories are present and each item matches its category	10 pts.	
Organization (1 pt.)	Bibliography is not in alphabetical order	0 pts.	
	Bibliography is partially in alphabetical order but some errors are present	.1–.9 pts.	
	Bibliography is in alphabetical order	1 pt.	
Consistency of Style (8 pts.)	Fewer than half of the citations are in the proper APA format	0–2 pts.	
	Some citations are in the proper format, but the quantity and/or type of errors present indicates a poor/fair understanding of the format	3–6 pts.	
	Most, if not all, citations are in proper format, with few to no errors	7–8 pts.	
Annotations (5 pts.)	No annotations given, or, if present, demonstrate little knowledge of the source described; annotations have numerous grammar and/or spelling errors	0–1 pts.	

Criteria	Description	Level	Score
	Annotations demonstrate some knowledge of the source described; annotations are descriptive rather than critical; some grammar and/or spelling errors	2–3 pts.	
	Annotations are thorough and show a firm grasp of the source's value; annotations are critical; contain few to no grammar and/or spelling errors	4–5 pts.	
Comments:			

**Figure 7–3 Annotated Bibliography Rubric
(Adapted from Susan E. Beck, New Mexico State University)**

Success with our annotated bibliography rubric has led us to develop a rubric for another course assignment. Students often feel uncertain about what is expected of them during their five-minute presentation at the end of the course, even though the presentation is explained in the course syllabus and verbally several times during the quarter. However, some students are nervous about oral presentations, and this anxiety seems to be blocking their understanding and acceptance of what the presentation entails. We decided to see if a rubric would help us with this assignment (Figure 7–4). While it has been in use for a much shorter period than the annotated bibliography rubric, initial signs show it is helping.

Another rubric from the same information literacy course is used to assess students' presentations given at the end of the course. Originality is not required, although it will be rewarded if present, so no points are deducted if a presentation lacks originality. Also, because this is not a public speaking course, points are not taken off for poor speaking skills, but listing them on the rubric emphasizes what good speaking skills involve.

Concept Maps

Concept maps, a form of cognitive assessment, can be used very effectively to assess student learning. They are frequently used for formative assessment purposes, but might also be used for summative purposes. Concept maps can be a very powerful classroom assessment technique. They allow you to see clearly how students are structuring their under-

Oral Presentation Rubric		
Final Oral Presentation (10 points)		
Criteria	Range	Score and comments
Content (7 points)	Little connection to bibliography topic or information sources for topic: 0–2 points Presentation leans heavily either on topic explanation OR on sources found/stumbling blocks encountered: 3–4 points Presentation balances topic and process of finding information: 5–7 points	Score: Comments:
Originality (extra point)	Nothing unusual: neutral Effective use of media or other resources: 1 bonus point (if under 10)	Score: Comments:
Timing (1 point)	Does not reach 5 minutes or is excessively long: 0 points 5 minutes (or slightly longer): 1 point	Score: Comments:
Outline (2 points)	No outline provided: 0 points Outline provided: 2 points	Score:
Speaking Skills (not graded)	You are encouraged to speak clearly and at a suitable volume, have good eye contact, be confident	Comments:
Figure 7–4 Oral Presentation Rubric		

standing of a concept or topic. They also require students to reflect upon what they know, and to determine how various aspects are connected.

> In creating concept maps, students singly or in groups can be presented with a central concept or principle, and they then generate subconcepts that relate to it, or the subconcepts can be supplied....Lines are then drawn linking the sub- and central concepts, with a brief explanation of what the link or relationship is. (Biggs, 1999: 82)

You can use concept maps in a variety of ways. You might ask students to draw a concept map of a major topic before you teach it, in order to gauge students' knowledge of the topic. If the knowledge is greater or less than you expected, you might alter your lesson to take this into account. You might ask students to map a particularly difficult topic just after it has been taught, to see where gaps in understanding occur. The tool can be used for summative assessment, to show students' understanding at the end of the course or at the end of a unit.

While an individual's concept of a topic is uniquely his or hers, there can be advantages to having students work on concept maps in small groups. Through their discussion, students have the opportunity to learn from their classmates. They may see connections or learn about subtopics that they themselves would not have thought of. In addition, drawing a concept map might be less intimidating to students when it is a shared activity, particularly if they have not encountered this technique before. Whether you ask students to develop their own concept maps or do them jointly, make sure that you explain what concept maps are and how they are drawn (stress the terms that show relationships between the links). Provide examples that illustrate other topics to clarify your explanations.

The described assignment takes approximately twenty minutes of class time. However, if you would like to use a concept map assessment and do not have this much class time available, assign one as homework. Or ask students to map a smaller topic that might not have as many subconcepts.

One of the authors uses a concept mapping exercise after the midpoint of the quarter. After explaining what concept maps are and sharing an example with students, she supplies them with a list of all the topics covered in the course to that point. She has students work in small groups to draw concept maps that they can all agree upon. She then asks a couple of groups to display their creations using the document camera while they explain why they drew the maps the way they did. This will usually generate productive discussion on a number of points that might have been unclear. It is also an excellent way for students to piece together various aspects of information literacy, and for the instructor to determine which parts and connections they understand well, and which they do not.

The concept mapping assignment described is shown in Figure 7-5

Exercise Example: Concept Mapping

Concept Mapping Exercise
These are the topics that we have studied in class so far. Please discuss these topics with the students in your group. Your goal is to develop a concept map such as the one that was just explained. In this concept map, you will show the relationships as you perceive them between the topics below. Use lines with brief explanations to describe the relationships.
Draw your concept map on a separate piece of paper. Be prepared to describe it to the rest of the class, using the document camera to display the concept map.

Information Literacy
Impact of Technology on Information
Data/Information/Knowledge/Wisdom
Research Process (feelings about)
Popular Periodicals vs. Scholarly Periodicals
Types of Libraries (Academic, Public, Special)
Topic Selection/Thesis Statements
Reference Sources
Citing Sources
Scholarly/Popular/Full-Text Articles
Print Indexes
Electronic Databases

Figure 7–5 Exercise Example: Concept Mapping

An example of the concept map students drew in response to this assignment is shown in Figure 7–6.

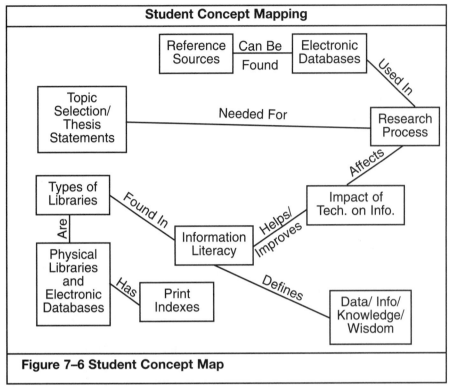

Figure 7–6 Student Concept Map

Returning to Montgomery's definition of authentic assessment, concept mapping allows students to demonstrate, in a meaningful way, what they know. It concentrates on holistic rather than discrete or isolated knowledge. In addition, it requires higher levels of cognitive thinking (Montgomery, 2002: 35).

Minute Writing

Another classroom assessment technique is minute writing or free writing. As implied by the name, minute writing exercises take little time. In minute writing, you ask students to spend a short period answering a question or two, or reflecting in some way on a topic. As mentioned in the section on Writing to Learn in Chapter 5, students generally do not write their names on the papers, in order to encourage them to be frank in their reflections and comments. In order for this form of assessment to be effective, it is not necessary to know whose paper is whose. However, should you like to provide personalized feedback to individual students, rather than to the class as a whole, you could ask them to put their names on their papers.

This assessment technique is extremely flexible. As with concept maps, minute writing can be done before instruction to determine student knowledge, or at other points during or following instruction to gauge student learning. It is useful for determining points that may be causing confusion. Minute writing might also be used at the start of a class to focus students on the subject, or to encourage them to recall what was learned in the previous class session.

Minute writing exercises ask students to think about topics in ways that they might not otherwise do. Depending upon what you are asking students to write, they may be able to identify for themselves gaps in their knowledge or topics about which they would like to learn more. In some cases, when you read over the responses, you will be able to find areas in which the class as a whole needs more instruction. Another way to follow up on minute writing is to have pairs or small groups of students share and discuss their individual responses. Regardless of the follow-up method, minute writing assessments lead to increased confidence on the part of students: either you or they will identify gaps between teaching and learning, and have the opportunity to bridge these gaps. Students will feel more confident that they are learning what they should, and that they will be prepared for more formal methods of assessment. This assessment technique lends itself well to two aspects of effective assessment: it is easy to

---

**Figure 7-7 Instructor Tip:
Minute Writing Examples**

There is a wide range of questions that can be used in minute writing. Any of the following can be adapted to the topic you are teaching. You are certain to think of a number of other questions that might be posed.

At the start of class or before starting a new topic:
- What are two questions you still have about [last class's topic]?
- What are three things you know to be true about [new topic of the day]?

During a class:
- What connections do you see between [topic] and [topic]?
- How do you envisage using [topic] while you are in college?
- How do you envisage using [topic] once you are in the workplace?
- How does [topic] compare to [topic]?

At the end of class:
- What is the main point you learned today?
- What was the main point left unanswered in today's session?
- What was the muddiest point [of a homework assignment/reading/lecture]? (Angelo and Cross, 1993: 154–158)

include it in your plans for ongoing assessment, particularly because it takes little time, and it is very adaptable, allowing you to integrate assessment with the rest of the course.

One of the authors once asked a class to write down the key point of that day's class. When she read through the entries and found that a majority of the students thought that Interlibrary Loan was the main point (it certainly wasn't meant to be!), she knew she had taken a wrong turn somewhere, and was able to change her emphasis in similar future classes. Without this very quick assessment tool, she would not have known that her instruction had not accomplished its goal.

Cases

Asking students to grapple with case studies has a multitude of motivational benefits. Some disciplines rarely or never use case studies, and this method will pique the interest of students accustomed to those disciplines. Cases should be designed to describe actual scenarios so they will rate high on the relevance scale. And, like other authentic assessment tools, cases can engender confidence and satisfaction on the part of students.

The case method is:

- Intended to further the development of professional intellectual and behavioral skills
- Issue — or problem — oriented
- Essentially concerned with interpreting real-world experience (Lynn, 1999: 3)

For cases to be effective teaching tools, they need to meet certain criteria:

> A case is a factual description of events that actually happened at some point in the past. Although fictional stories may meet some pedagogical objectives, they do not have the intellectual rigor of a case based in factual research. The case is designed to meet specific pedagogical or research objectives of the case writer. As such, the case must provide sufficient material concerning the situation and the environment surrounding it to meet those objectives. (Naumes and Naumes, 1999: 10)

Naumes and Naumes point out that some students are uncomfortable with the ambiguous nature of cases. They prefer situations where there is one correct answer (Naumes and Naumes, 1999: 11). In order that this concern not undermine students' confidence, it is important to talk about this feature of cases with them. It would also be a good idea, if you plan to use cases for summative assessment, to allow students to practice on a case in class so that they become more familiar with what is expected of them.

The complexity and length of cases will vary depending upon your intent. A case that you use as an in-class assessment technique might be less complex than a case you use for summative assessment as a final course project. For in-depth advice on the use and writing of cases, the books by Lynn and Naumes and Naumes are excellent resources.

For one example of a case that could be used in an information literacy course, see Figure 7–8.

Intellectual Property Case Study

Abstract:

The information literacy classroom is the ideal place to explore the topic of intellectual property by raising questions about authorship, originality, copyright, appropriation, and plagiarism. When discussing these issues, it is important to do more than simply tell students that it is wrong to plagiarize. Most students already know this, but they may be less clear about why it is so crucial to document all sources, especially when they have such easy access to visual, textual, and aural information in digital environments. Of course, it is vital to have clear policies in place to explain the consequences of plagiarism. We also need to provide students with the practical skills needed to look critically at a range of information sources, evaluate those sources, write effectively based on their research, and properly document all sources.

At the same time, it is essential to provide students with a larger framework to explore intellectual property in digital environments. Developing case studies that address these issues may encourage class discussions based on these interconnected themes. This may enable students to gain a deeper understanding about what plagiarism is and how to prevent it. The case study that follows, entitled *The Banner*, challenges students to think about originality and the creative process. This case study presents a situation that may be difficult to resolve. Students are encouraged to think about authorship, originality, ethics, appropriation, and copyright within a professional business context of Web-based multimedia advertising.

Perhaps the most difficult aspect of this particular case involves the way we understand and define the ownership of ideas. In the classroom, students very often raise questions and concerns about citing ideas in academic work. Although the rules for citing direct quotes may seem obvious to many students, documenting ideas and theories in academic writing

Figure 7–8 Intellectual Property Case Study (Thomas P. Mackey, University at Albany)

very often presents the class with a gray area that may be difficult to define or understand. Many students express concerns about the unintentional plagiarism of key concepts and raise questions about whether or not any idea is truly original. The purpose of this case study is to explore this gray area with a particular focus on the transient and virtual environment of Web space.

The Banner

With over five years of part-time Web development experience and a degree in Digital Media, Andre landed the perfect job. Mirage.com was one of the few startups in Manhattan that survived the dot-com bubble. As a trendy advertising company, Mirage.com built a solid reputation for original and creative multimedia Web development for some of the biggest names in corporate advertising. This business not only survived difficult economic times, but prospered because *the look* of a Mirage.com Web site and advertisement is always distinctive.

Andre loves cars as much as Web development and he was thrilled to lead the animation design team for automotive advertising. Andre worked with a team of Web developers and designers to create graphics, logos, and animation for several car companies. He created eye-catching banner and pop-up ads that appeared on a number of high-profile Web sites. Banner ads are usually seen in the header or side margins of a Web site and pop-up ads appear any time a user clicks on a site or a specific Web page. Banner and pop-up ads are animated with text and graphics, and some of the best ones include sound. One of the reasons for the success of Mirage.com, even in a difficult economy, was due in part to the lucrative sales of these animated advertisements. Banners and pop-ups are everywhere on the Web, and as annoying as they may be to some users, Mirage.com research indicates that this form of Web advertising is highly effective. People claim that they do not like these ads, but they tend to remember the names of the products advertised.

In his second year at Mirage.com, Andre was faced with a professional crisis that placed his status with the company in jeopardy. It also challenged the way he thought about the creative process. On a Friday afternoon Andre was called into the office of the CEO of Mirage.com, Jon Stevens, the founder and original designer of the company's early award-winning ads and Web sites. Jon and Andre always worked well together and Andre admired the way Jon ran the company. Jon has a way of motivating the employees at Mirage.com with all kinds of perks and a nontraditional work environment that allows the employees to telecommute, wear whatever they want in the office, bring their pets to work, and spend at least an hour a day at the gym. Jon was all about creativity and nurturing an open environment for new ideas. He was as comfortable talking with his employees about the advantages of yoga and a healthy diet, as he was discussing the creative potential of the latest multimedia software. Andre flourished in this atmosphere and was constantly generating unique visual ideas for his ads.

The person Andre admired most was suddenly raising questions about his originality. Jon informed Andre that the company was being sued for

Figure 7-8 continued

copyright infringement because of a banner ad Andre designed for the new Sportster SUV LX. The Sportster was one of the first sport utility vehicles marketed to consumers as reasonably priced, safe, luxurious, and highly efficient in terms of gas mileage. Andre developed a visually stunning banner ad targeting environmentally-conscious young professionals who wanted a solid SUV that was also safe, affordable, and trendy. The ad was intended to put consumers at ease about the safety concerns of SUVs, as well as the high cost of similar vehicles by other manufacturers.

Andre's approach was fairly simple but inventive. He created a visual effect that transformed a military tank into the new Sportster SUV LX. The tank moves from the left part of the banner to the right as it transforms into the new SUV, and then moves out of the frame entirely. After this fast-paced animation the banner text reads: *We change you. Sportster SUV LX.* While this visual and textual transformation takes place, an old song by David Bowie called *Changes* plays in the background. Andre's idea was to illustrate a new way of looking at the sport utility vehicle. The visual transformation from the tank to the Sportster demonstrates a change in the way people think about SUVs. While this vehicle is solid, tough, and safe, it is also sporty, fun, and economical. The text suggests that the consumer will also change if they buy one.

Although Andre admitted that he appropriated the Bowie song from a peer-to-peer music site, and the image of the tank from the U.S. Army site, he was surprised to learn from Jon that this is not the reason for the lawsuit. Andre immediately defended the use of the song and the image because he considered the banner a prototype for a more extensive campaign to follow. Although what he did was against company policy, he told Jon that he didn't think it would be necessary to receive official approval for the song or the image at this point since the banner ad only ran on a few test sites. Jon replied: "Well, we are not being sued by Bowie or the Army, only because they probably don't know about this, but we are being sued by the makers of the *Journey SUV,* because they claim you stole their idea." Andre immediately responded: "Stole their idea? My banner is completely original."

Apparently the banner ad for the Journey SUV also involves a multimedia transformation effect and similar phrasing to Andre's ad. In the Journey ad, a huge classic car from the 1950s transforms into the sleek new *Journey SUV,* and the text reads: *Change with us. Journey SUV.* The instrumental music used in the banner for the Journey SUV is entirely original and produced especially for the ad campaign.

The ad agency that developed the banner for the Journey SUV is suing Mirage.com for copyright infringement because they believe the concept for their ad was stolen. They argue that the visual idea used in their ad is unique to their client's vehicle and that the phrasing in the Sportster SUV LX banner is too similar to the text they wrote. The makers of the Journey SUV targeted the same audience as the Sportster SUV, and the features of the Journey are similar as well: reasonable price, excellent gas mileage, convenience, and safety. Central to their ad campaign is the idea that the Journey will change the way people think about SUVs. They argue that the Journey SUV offers consumers something new and that the Sportster ad takes away from their original con-

Figure 7-8 continued

cept. From their point of view the visual transformation that takes place in the banner is intended to suggest a change in the way consumers understand SUVs and how they will change as individuals once they purchase one. This is a new generation SUV for young consumers. The visual information is integral to the concept they are trying to communicate. The ad campaign for the Journey started at least three months earlier than the Sportster ad.

Andre has found himself at the center of a legal and ethical controversy that threatens to damage the reputation of Mirage.com as an innovative, original, and creative advertising startup on the cutting edge of new Web technologies. He admits that he should have been more careful about appropriating the Bowie song and U.S. Army image, but he is stunned that the reason for the lawsuit has to do with a visual idea. He acknowledges that he probably did see the Journey SUV ad at some point, since he surfs the Web all the time, but he has no awareness whatsoever of stealing the idea for the ad. He even told Jon that he didn't really care for the Journey ad, and he doesn't see the similarity that the makers of the Journey claim.

As Andre sits in Jon's office, he considers the complex set of issues surrounding his simple banner ad, and the impact this may have on Mirage.com, his future, and maybe the way he designs and creates. Now that Jon has explained the case, Andre continues to raise the same question: "How is it possible to steal an idea?"

Discussion Questions:

1. Did Andre steal the idea for his banner ad from the Journey SUV banner?
2. Is there any way Andre could have acknowledged the influence of the original ad in this context?
3. Is it possible that Andre stole the idea unintentionally? If so, is he still responsible?
4. Is Mirage.com responsible in any way for what happened?
5. Is Andre guilty of copyright infringement for appropriating the image of the tank from the U.S. Army Web site and the sound file from the David Bowie song? If either Bowie or the Army finds out about the appropriation, do you think Mirage.com will be sued again? Should they be?
6. Is it possible to plagiarize images and sounds?
7. Is it possible to plagiarize ideas?
8. If an image or sound is available on the Web, does this mean anyone can use it for any purpose?
9. Is it possible to plagiarize outside of academic environments?
10. How should this matter be resolved?

Figure 7-8 continued

Portfolios

Portfolios are an excellent example of authentic assessment. Using Montgomery's definition of authentic assessment at the start of this chapter, portfolios meet these criteria:

- They demonstrate what students know and are able to do.
- They do not measure discrete, isolated skills.
- They involve the holistic performance of complex tasks.
- They are multidimensional.
- They require higher levels of cognitive thinking.

What exactly is a portfolio?

> A portfolio is a purposeful collection of student work that exhibits the student's efforts, progress, and achievements in one or more areas. The collection must include student participation in selecting contents, the criteria for selection, the criteria for judging merit, and evidence of student self-reflection. (Paulson, Paulson, and Meyer: 1991: 60)

Portfolios might be very appropriate for information literacy courses that last long enough for students to produce, reflect upon, and collect the material that will make up the portfolio. Initial drafts as well as the corresponding finished product may be included to demonstrate a student's progress; seeing these items side by side can provide a strong boost to a student's confidence and satisfaction over a job well done.

While portfolios might not be appropriate in courses of short duration, they work well in semester-long information literacy and research courses. A librarian and a professor at SUNY New Paltz include a portfolio assignment in their Bibliographic Research in Music course. Information about their portfolio and the grading rubric is given in Figure 7–9.

Portfolio Assignment, SUNY New Paltz

Bibliographic Research in Music
Grading: Individual projects will be assessed for quality and neatness, but will not be formally graded. To receive a final grade, students will assemble a portfolio.

These portfolio elements are required:
- A digital video of the student's lecture/demo (instructor-created)
- A Webliography (in MLA 5 format)
- Two rubric checklists for the lecture/demo (instructors)
- Final abstract
- Final concert notes
- Library assignment
- Concert notes bibliography (in MLA 5 style)

These portfolio elements are optional:
- Relevant e-mail sent to the instructors, or to fellow students
- Personal reflections on course readings
- Critiques of fellow students' writings
- Drafts, working copies

- Additional bibliographies, abstracts, critiques, etc., prepared by the student
- Critiques by fellow students
- Relevant multimedia materials

The instructors and the student will jointly determine the final grade, based upon the quality of the portfolio. The following scale will be used:

To receive an A: Student portfolios must include all of the required elements, completed neatly and according to individual assignment parameters, and include substantial optional work (i.e., at least five optional pieces).

To receive a B+: Student portfolios must include all of the required elements, completed neatly and according to individual assignment parameters, and include optional work (but less than five pieces).

To receive a B: Student portfolios must include all of the required elements, completed neatly and according to individual assignment parameters, but include no optional work.

Portfolios that are missing required elements, or ones that have elements with a substantial number of errors, will receive a grade to be determined by the instructors in consultation with the student.

Students will maintain their own portfolios (on floppy disk(s) if possible.) Disk(s) and paperwork will be collected at the end of the semester.

Peer Review: Student work (e.g., drafts) will be subject to class critique. Students are responsible for generating paper copies for the instructors, as well as a machine-readable copy of all documents for use in class. Student work will be reviewed by classmates, who will put their critiques in writing if requested. All enrolled students are required to participate in peer review!

**Figure 7–9 Portfolio Assignment, SUNY New Paltz
(Mumper and Macaluso, 2002)**

A distance education research information skills module taught in South Africa asks students to include the following items in their portfolio:

- A selection of sources
- A search strategy
- An explanation of how the search results were evaluated
- Search results displayed in a format that could be included in a personal database
- A personal database with fields that will help students compile a bibliography
- The addition of 25–50 records to the database
- Proof that they have evaluated the database according to criteria for a bibliography in their discipline
- A bibliography which meets the requirements for their discipline (Fourie and van Niekerk, 1999: 343)

Fourie and van Niekerk very explicitly lay out the advantages of using a portfolio in their research information skills module, the pedagogical benefits, the necessary components, and methods for assessing the product (Fourie and van Niekerk, 1999). The authors highly recommend this article for those who would like to include portfolio assessment in their information literacy courses.

Assistance with Authentic Assessment

If you are looking for additional ideas about actual authentic assessment tools or for assistance in implementing them in your course, consider some of the following resources:

- Other librarians teaching information literacy courses, either at your institution or elsewhere
- Faculty members at your institution who are using authentic assessment in other courses
- The center for teaching, if there is one on your campus

Start slowly as you implement authentic assessment into your course. You may be able to enhance a current assignment by developing a rubric for it. You might easily add several minute writing exercises over the course of the term. Remember the principles of effective assessment mentioned earlier in the chapter, and keep in mind your comfort level with change. The success you have with small enhancements will give you the experience and confidence to tackle larger changes.

References

Angelo, Thomas A., and K. Patricia Cross. 1993. *Classroom Assessment Techniques: A Handbook for College Teachers*. 2nd ed. San Francisco: Jossey-Bass.

Beck, Susan E. 2001. "Meta-Learning Research Project." In *Teaching Information Literacy Concepts: Activities and Frameworks from the Field*, edited by Trudi E. Jacobson and Timothy H. Gatti. Pittsburgh: Library Instruction Publications.

Biggs, John. 1999. *Teaching for Quality Learning at University*. Buckingham, UK: Society for Research into Higher Education and Open University Press.

Forsyth, Donelson R., and James H. McMillan. 1991. "Practical Proposals for Motivating Students." In *College Teaching: From Theory to Practice*, edited by Robert J. Menges and Marilla D. Svinicki. *New Directions for Teaching and Learning*, no. 45 (Spring): 53–65.

Fourie, Ina, and Daleen van Niekerk. 1999. "Using Portfolio Assessment in a Module in Research Information Skills." *Education for Information* 17: 333–352.

Keller, John M. 1987. "Strategies for Stimulating the Motivation to Learn." *Performance and Instruction* 26, no. 8 (October): 1–7.

Lynn, Laurence E., Jr. 1999. *Teaching and Learning with Cases: A Guidebook*. New York: Chatham House.

Montgomery, Kathleen. 2002. "Authentic Tasks and Rubrics: Going Beyond Traditional Assessments in College Teaching." *College Teaching* 50, no. 1 (Winter): 34–39.

Mumper, Robert, and Stephan J. Macaluso. 2002. "Course Syllabus: Bibliographic Research in Music." (April 2003)
Available:http://www2.newpaltz.edu/~macaluss/acrl_music_class/66430.doc

Naumes, William, and Margaret J. Naumes. 1999. *The Art and Craft of Case Writing*. Thousand Oaks, CA: Sage.

Paulson, F. Leon, Pearl R. Paulson, and Carol A. Meyer. 1991. "What Makes a Portfolio a Portfolio?" *Educational Leadership* 48, no. 5 (February): 60–63.

Pickett, Nancy, and Bernie Dodge. 2001. "Rubrics for Web Lessons." (March 2003)
Available: http://webquest.sdsu.edu/rubrics/weblessons.htm

Reeves, Thomas C. 2000. "Alternative Assessment Approaches for Online Learning Environments in Higher Education." *Journal of Educational Computing Research* 23, no. 1: 101–111.

Schrock, Kathy. 2002. "Kathy Schrock's Guide for Educators: Assessment and Rubric Information." (March 2003) Available:
http://school.discovery.com/schrockguide/assess.html

Chapter 8
Online Teaching Situations

Some information literacy courses are taught entirely online, while others, which meet in a more traditional manner, incorporate Web-based teaching elements. While a number of the motivational elements of classroom instruction are applicable in courses that are wholly or partially Web-based, there are motivation-enhancing components that are unique to this electronic setting.

Many authors who write about online instruction stress that this mode of teaching works well with motivated, independent learners. Adult learners with a very specific goal in mind are often cited as learners who are more likely to succeed in online courses. Time management skills and a willingness to take responsibility for their own learning are critical for students enrolled in such courses.

However, those who teach online information literacy courses will find a diverse array of students enrolled in their courses, not just those likely to succeed in this alternative learning environment. As the instructor, you can include a number of elements that will enhance student motivation and learning.

Features of Online Instruction

Keller identifies three key characteristics of online instruction that can challenge both students and instructors: learners are "typically isolated—in space if not in time"; they "normally have to work for long periods without social reinforcement"; and they "have to be able to learn effectively from text and graphics" (Keller, 1999: 2, 10).

Students in online courses do not see their professor and fellow students, nor do they generally work synchronously with them. This is certainly not to say that they do not interact with them: many online courses include discussion sessions, and frequently courses that do meet in the classroom have an electronic discussion feature. But students who are learning while sitting in front of their computers may feel the sense of isolation that Keller mentions, and it is up to you, as the instructor, to mitigate it. You are also able to structure the course so that students will receive reinforcement both from you and from fellow students. In order to shift the focus from the text and graphics on the screen to the people and ideas behind them, the inclusion of discussion, active learning, and application exercises are important. In this chapter, we examine a number of methods to enhance motivation to learn that take into account, and overcome, some of the challenging characteristics of online instruction.

ARCS Motivation Model and Online Teaching Situations

Grabowski and Curtis adapted Keller's four motivational factors for use in hypermedia environments:

- Interest in or attention to the information and the technology;
- Perceived relevance of the information;
- Self-confidence in the ability to access and use the information; and
- Resulting satisfaction from successful access to and usefulness of the information (Grabowski and Curtis, 1991: 10).

These revised factors emphasize the student's ability to use the technology involved successfully. If students are not able to access and use all required electronic elements of the course, they will find their frustration overwhelming their initial motivation. It is important that students have easy access to technological support, either through the instructor, or, more likely, through the institution. Some students enjoy tackling and mastering new software that might be used in an online course. Others simply see it as a hurdle that has to be overcome before they can get on with what they want to learn. While these students will not fit the above category of interest in the technology, instructors should make sure their attention to it is not due to technical problems.

Technical issues aside, online instruction has the ability to gain students' attention because of its format, particularly if a student is not already familiar with online courses. However, if the instruction is poorly conceived or executed, this benefit may be lost. Just as with instruction accomplished in a physical classroom, relevance is critically important for motivating students. The material must be relevant to their course of study, to their goals beyond college, and, when possible, to their daily interests. It must also be designed to encourage student confidence, and to be challenging yet achievable, so that students feel a sense of satisfaction. Online teaching situations offer some actual or perceived obstacles to students that may temper students' motivation. These factors will be addressed in the following sections.

Techniques for Increasing Motivation in Online Classes

In order to increase student motivation in online classes, instructors will need to use a combination of techniques already discussed in this book, such as offering a variety of challenges, actively engaging students, and providing students with autonomy, along with a number of additional techniques that specifically address features of online instruction. The following techniques adapt and build upon ideas mentioned earlier in this book, and provide a number of new ideas suitable for the online setting.

Course Design

If you are adapting an existing information literacy course that has been taught in the classroom for use as an online course, you will need to rethink a number of the course elements that affect student motivation. Simply putting all your lectures and assignments on the Web is not sufficient. It is critical to learn what is needed for a successful online course, either through reading about others' experiences or through talking to those who have done it. You will certainly be able to use many of your existing materials, but you will need to modify and supplement them, and to design new activities.

When you construct the course syllabus, assignments, and other written materials, scrutinize them for clarity. This is important for traditionally-taught courses, but is absolutely critical for online courses. Because you are not right there in the classroom with the students, it is harder for students to ask questions about what you mean, and time will be lost in waiting for your response. Decide upon and clearly explain communication methods and schedules. Responsibilities, deadlines, and other requirements should be spelled out completely. Let students know how you will communicate with them and establish a schedule. Will you use a Web site or e-mail for assignments?

When will you post or send assignments? Because students need to fit this online work into their own schedules and need to know what to expect, you must be consistent in the method you use and the timing you promise (Nader, 2001). Motivation will plummet if students do not know where to look for the materials you send, or do not receive them when expected.

Examine your course's goals and objectives carefully. Consider the online instructional medium and how it will affect the goals, objectives, and student learning outcomes. While many instructors of classroom sections will stress that they expect students to be engaged, you might want to be more specific with an online course. As an example, you might tell students that you expect them to contribute at least twice a week to the course discussion, and that one of these messages should synthesize or evaluate material found in others' messages. A number of students in your course may be new to online instruction. It will help them if you are very specific about what you expect of your students, and what their level of participation needs to be for them to be successful in your online course. This degree of detail will enable students to gauge how they are doing in this perhaps unfamiliar setting.

Experienced teachers of online courses emphasize the need to be extremely explicit about the quantity and quality of the responses that you expect from students. Provide individual students with a critique of their responses after the first week so that they will be very clear about how their work meets your expectations.

Design your online course so that you use a variety of learning activities. "From a motivational perspective, the learning environment must have features that both get and sustain student attention. To 're-energize' the students from time to time, it is necessary to provide variation in sequencing and types of activities" (Keller, 1999: 10). This is important, and perhaps easier to envisage, in a traditional classroom, but it is crucial in an online course as well. Several types of activities that can be used are described at the end of this chapter.

Relevance is a key component of motivation. Relevance of the course material is particularly critical in online courses, where student motivation may be the deciding factor on whether students drop the course or make the necessary time in their schedule to complete it. Examine your topics and examples carefully—is there a way to make them more interesting to students while still meeting your goals?

Teaching Behaviors/Instructor Presence

Seen from both a student's perspective (Priest, 2000) and an educator's perspective (Bischoff, 2000), the way an instructor interacts with an online class has an effect on students' learning and motivation. Teachers must:

- establish their presence
- be accessible
- make the online environment friendly
- communicate clearly and effectively
- be visible to their students
- provide useful feedback

In the physical classroom, an instructor's presence is not an issue. As an instructor in the online environment, where you cannot rely on visual cues for student interaction and feedback, it is vital for you to establish your presence in other ways. This can be done through the messages you send to students and through online discussions, which will be addressed in more depth in a separate section below. If students do not feel that you are present, listening in, and monitoring their work, they will begin to wonder why they are bothering to do the work, and motivation may plummet. They will also expect you to keep discussions on track, and to intervene quickly to address any problems of flaming. By making yourself visible to the students, you are also modeling the level of participation you would like of them (Bischoff, 2000: 61).

Bischoff suggests using a variety of types of messages to make you visible: content-related messages (connected to the intellectual material of the course), process-related messages (such as explaining assignments or providing guidance to confused students), technical tips, protocol guidelines (code of conduct, plagiarism statement), and responses to students (Bischoff, 2000: 60).

Make sure you are accessible to your students. Instructors always provide contact information on their syllabus. Students may not make use of it as often as we would like, but it is there. For in-person classes, instructors provide office location, phone number, and e-mail address. Be sure to do the same for online courses. The inclination may be to think that students will only use e-mail. However, e-mail does not serve all purposes. Let them know how to get you "live." Also, do not expect that students will need less help and less of your time because they are doing some of the coursework independently. Not only will you need to answer questions about the course content, assignments, and other aspects, as you would for a traditional course, you will also be asked about the method being used to deliver the course, and the procedures for discussion and interaction, how students are to submit materials, etc.

In order to create a friendly and personalized online atmosphere, which helps to get students' attention, Nader suggests e-mails to the whole class or to individuals to "emulate the social interaction of the classroom." This might include using a greeting line and a distinct class signature file, mentioning campus or news events, using stories as ice breakers, praising work well done by the class, or sending relevant URLs. Adapt those techniques that you use and feel comfortable with in a traditional classroom (Nader, 2001).

> One instructor of an online course sends a regular end-of-the-week letter to students with her responses to their comments that week, incorporating key quotes from their messages. This weekly letter, which combines Bischoff's categories of content-related messages and responses to students, reassures students that their professor is indeed present and carefully reading their contributions.

Online instruction offers an advantage in respect to small group work. While you can only listen in on one classroom group at a time, you can monitor the work of all online groups. Be careful about being too intrusive into the work each group is doing, but regular acknowledgement that you are there and listening will be valued by students.

Assessment/Feedback

In many courses, grades are not based on performances on tests and assignments alone. Student participation is often an important factor in assessing student learning and in grading. Students are often able to determine the quality of their in-class participation through the way instructors react and use their comments and responses. Students in online courses cannot gauge how they are doing in the course by these same informal methods. This relates to the lack of social reinforcement that Keller included in his features of online instruction (1999). It is vital that instructors of online courses be aware of students' need for feedback in order to maintain or enhance their motivation.

Bischoff describes the importance of using feedback, and emphasizes that it must be provided to the entire class, as well as to individual students. "Frequent and consistent feedback in the online classroom can stimulate active engagement by techniques such as questioning assumptions, disagreeing with certain points, and pointing out well-analyzed points….Giving feedback in the main meeting includes asking questions, suggesting alternative perspectives to consider, and extending on students' ideas" (Bischoff, 2000: 62). Because online courses move quickly, "feedback that is timely is far more motivational and beneficial to performance improvement than delayed feedback" (Bischoff, 2000: 63).

In Chapter 7, "Authentic Assessment," we examined the use of rubrics for assessing student learning on projects and other assignments. Bischoff suggests the use of a template to provide weekly feedback to each student in an online course about his or her performance (Bischoff, 2000: 65). This technique addresses the isolation that students may feel, and also may bolster their self-confidence and satisfaction. Without regular feedback, students may feel very uncertain about their performance in the class. Bischoff's form indicates how many points a student received for discussion, participation, the week's essay, and the weekly summary, along with the number of possible points for each. She also provides each student with his or her total points for the week, and a brief personal message about each student's work. Such a template might easily be adapted for information literacy courses. If the elements remain stable from week to week, it might be used in conjunction with a rubric or guide that indicates how each item is graded.

Weekly quizzes, short writing projects, and case studies, as discussed in Chapter 7, are equally pertinent in online courses. Portfolios might also be used, and could be made available online, given the nature of the course. Additional information on the assessment of student learning in the online environment, including comparisons with assessment in the traditional environment and a selection of appropriate assessment techniques, is found in Jacobson (2003).

Gauging Student Background/Enhancing Student Awareness

Powers and Guan state, "Three factors have been reported to help identify students' motivation [in distance learning]: intention to complete the course, early submission of work, and completion of other distance education courses" (Powers and Guan, 2000: 205). They suggest obtaining information on these and other factors through the use of an online questionnaire, administered before or at the start of the course. The questionnaire might ask students for demographic and academic data, information on previous experience with the subject and the method of instruction, reasons for taking the course, perceptions of the method of instruction, anxieties about the method, identification of learning style, interpersonal orientation, time management, and strategies that students think might help them succeed in this course. Powers and Guan suggest that this information might then be used "not only as a database for the instructional designer to conduct a learner analysis, but also a reminder for the learners to be more aware of or alert to their potential barriers" (Powers and Guan, 2000: 205).

Keller suggests enhancing student awareness as well.

> It can be helpful to acquaint students with the concepts of self-motivation and self-regulation, and to provide tactics that support these motivational perspectives. For example, one might include a goal-setting activity in web-based instruction that asks students to reflect on (1) their goals, (2) factors that will assist them in sustaining their motivation, (3) motivational obstacles that they will encounter, and (4) how they will overcome the obstacles. This type of thinking is characteristic of people who are high in need for achievement and has long been used in achievement motivation workshops. It seems to be particularly applicable in this setting. (Keller, 1999: 10)

Foregrounding issues of motivation, time management, and technology will enhance students' understanding of the importance these items play in an online course, and the need for them to take responsibility in ways they might not need to in traditional courses.

Conducting Discussions

Electronic discussions are extremely important in online courses. They help to mitigate issues of isolation and social reinforcement, require students to construct and verbalize knowledge, and serve as a means for instructors to assess student understanding and learning. In addition, online discussions provide a venue for encouraging students to think critically.

> Critical thinking, defined broadly as a dialogical process that produces an increasingly sound, well-grounded, and valid understanding of a topic or issue, involves participants developing and examining their ideas as fully as possible, presenting them clearly and credibly to others, and examining and challenging the ideas of others. In other words, critical thinking happens in good discussions. (Lang, 2000: 21)

There are a number of advantages to online discussions as compared to their oral counterparts. Written contributions can be reviewed and revised before they are shared with others, all online participants have a chance to be heard, and the extended time span of an online discussion can lead to more thoughtful exchanges (Lang, 2000: 21). Students who are expected to contribute in a meaningful way to class discussions will be challenged in ways they would not if discussion contributions were only expected to show knowledge or comprehension. Students will be motivated to show themselves off favorably to their classmates through the quality of their thinking and their writing (Lang, 2000: 21). Providing feedback to discussion contributors will help to boost students' confidence in their contributions and their satisfaction with the discussion sessions. Students who may be uncomfortable speaking up in class may be more willing to contribute in an online environment.

Lang cites a numbers of ways to encourage critical thinking in online discussions, including not lecturing; being clear about expectations; being responsive; monitoring and prompting for participation; writing summarizing comments every week or two; setting rules and standards; and establishing clear norms for participation and procedures for grading (Lang, 2000: 24).

A professor who has a great deal of experience teaching online courses encourages her students to answer other students' questions posted to the discussion forum. Student engagement is increased, while critical thinking is promoted.

While it is important to maintain a presence during an online discussion, think carefully about your role in it. Badger lists two possible pitfalls: dominating the discussion and encouraging those students who respond with what they think you want to hear (Badger, 2000: 132). Maintain a presence, but do not contribute in such a manner that students think you have put in the final word on a topic, cutting off other discussion.

Application Exercises with Feedback

Students in online courses need to have an opportunity to try out what they have learned. In traditional classes, instructors may have some hands-on exercises, either within or outside of class, that students can use to gauge how they are doing. It is important to include these application exercises in online courses as well. Without these opportunities, it is easy for students' confidence to flounder. Frequent exercises, together with the opportunity to see how they are doing, can boost students' confidence and satisfaction levels. Besides exercises that you assign to the entire class, consider providing additional, optional exercises with answer guides for students who prefer more opportunities to test their learning.

Problem-Based Learning

A variety of the active learning methods described in Chapter 5 can be translated to the online setting. In addition, problem-based learning is well-suited to this medium. This type of learning asks students to tackle real-life problems and situations that people encounter. "Problem-based learning is a curriculum approach which helps the learner frame experience as a series of problems to be solved and where the process of learning unfolds through the application of knowledge and skills to the solution of real-world problems, often in the contexts of real practice" (Oliver and Herrington, 2000: 183). Problem-based learning has been found to be a powerful way to motivate students, to increase critical thinking and problem-solving skills, and to help students to understand content (Sage and Torp, 1997: 32).

The following quote from Sage and Torp highlights the information aspect of problem-based learning, pointing out its value for information literacy courses, but also indicates other benefits:

> Because problem-based learning encourages students to explore information in different ways—through print, telephone, the Internet, etc.—and to learn about authentic problems, teachers believed it was also a motivating strategy for students with varied learning styles and strengths. (Sage and Torp, 1997: 34)

Authentic problems often have multiple solutions, lend themselves to multiple perspectives, and help students to anticipate the types of learning necessary for the workplace (Oliver and Herrington, 2000: 184). In an online teaching situation, students can be divided into small groups to work on actual problems that the instructor provides. Oliver and Herrington describe weekly problem-solving activities used in a Web-based course that might jump-start ideas about how to use this method in an information literacy course.

> The weekly problem is given in the on-line course notes along with a number of initial references and information sources, both online and in print. Students are expected to read the various sources and consider an appropriate solution. The students can then meet together to plan their problem-solving strategies; many, however, prefer to use e-mail for this purpose....The students work together to solve the problem,

some collecting information, others analyzing the problem setting and considering the options. A solution is developed with a word limit of 250 words. The students pass this between themselves to polish and refine it. At the end of the week, the solution is posted. (Oliver and Herrington, 2000: 186)

These posted solutions can be seen by all students in the class; indeed, they are expected to read them and to select the best solutions from all those submitted.

In an information literacy course, this model might be adapted to have students actually find appropriate information sources once they have learned enough to do so. One or two groups might be responsible for finding the sources for all groups to use for each individual problem. The problems themselves might revolve around social and ethical issues connected to the use of information. Problems based on situations involving plagiarism, privacy, and copyright would all be appropriate to use. Discipline-specific courses online might easily adapt problems from within the discipline. Students will find that the real-world nature of the problems makes learning exciting and motivating.

Assistance with Online Teaching

Adapting a traditional course to the online environment or developing a new online course can be challenging, particularly if you are new to this method of teaching. You may have a number of questions, not all of which are related to motivation. Connect with other instructors who have taught online. They will be fonts of information about what to expect, what worked, and what did not. You might even be able to audit one of their existing online courses. If you have access to a teaching center, its staff may be very helpful in pointing you toward experienced online instructors. It might also be willing to set up a session in which a number of online instructors can share their experiences, or even a full-fledged workshop in which those new to the online environment can get practical help developing an online course.

Many of the motivational techniques described throughout this book can be used effectively in the online setting. As you gain expertise teaching online information literacy courses, consider sharing your techniques for motivating students with other instructors, through conference presentations and publications.

References

Badger, Al. 2000. "Keeping It Fun and Relevant: Using Active Learning Online." In *The Online Teaching Guide: A Handbook of Attitudes, Strategies, and Techniques for the Virtual Classroom*, edited by Ken W. White and Bob H. Weight. Boston: Allyn and Bacon.

Bischoff, Anita. 2000. "The Elements of Effective Online Teaching: Overcoming the Barriers to Success." In *The Online Teaching Guide: A Handbook of Attitudes, Strategies, and Techniques for the Virtual Classroom*, edited by Ken W. White and Bob H. Weight. Boston: Allyn and Bacon.

Grabowski, Barbara L., and Ruth Curtis. 1991. "Information, Instruction and Learning: A Hypermedia Perspective." *Performance Improvement Quarterly* 4, no. 3: 2–12.

Jacobson, Trudi E. 2003. "Assessment of Learning." In *Developing Web-Based Instruction: Planning, Designing, Managing, and Evaluating for Results*, edited by Elizabeth Dupuis. New York: Neal-Schuman.

Keller, John M. 1999. "Motivation in Cyber Learning Environments." Paper presented at the Korean Society for Educational Technology, May 30, in Seoul, Korea.

Lang, David. 2000. "Critical Thinking in Web Courses: An Oxymoron?" *Syllabus* 14, no. 2 (September): 20–21, 23–24.

Nader, Nadine. "Structuring, Formatting, and Organizing Online Assignments." University Center, MI: Delta College. (August, 2001) Available: www.delta.edu/annader/mentor.

Oliver, Ron, and Jan Herrington. 2000. "Using Situated Learning as a Design Strategy for Web-Based Learning." In *Instructional and Cognitive Impacts of Web-Based Education*, edited by Beverly Abbey. Hershey, PA: Idea Group.

Powers, Susan M., and Sharon Guan. 2000. "Examining the Range of Student Needs in the Design and Development of a Web-Based Course." In *Instructional and Cognitive Impacts of Web-Based Education*, edited by Beverly Abbey. Hershey, PA: Idea Group.

Priest, Lorraine. 2000. "The Story of One Learner: A Student's Perspective on Online Teaching." In *The Online Teaching Guide: A Handbook of Attitudes, Strategies, and Techniques for the Virtual Classroom*, edited by Ken W. White and Bob H. Weight. Boston: Allyn and Bacon.

Sage, Sara M. and Linda T. Torp. 1997. "What Does it Take to Become a Teacher of Problem-Based Learning?" *Journal of Staff Development* 18, no. 4: 32–36.

Index

About the Authors

Trudi E. Jacobson (tjacobson@uamail.albany.edu) is the Coordinator of User Education Programs at the University at Albany, SUNY, and an adjunct faculty member at the School of Information Science and Policy at the same institution. She coordinates and teaches the undergraduate Information Literacy courses, which reach approximately 1,000 freshmen and sophomores each year. Her professional interests include the use of critical thinking and active learning activities in the classroom. She is the coeditor of *Teaching the New Library to Today's Users* (Neal-Schuman, 2000) and *Teaching Information Literacy Concepts: Activities and Frameworks from the Field* (Library Instruction Publications, 2001), and editor of *Critical Thinking and the Web: Teaching Users to Evaluate Internet Resources* (Library Instruction Publications, 2000). She has published articles in a number of journals, including *The Journal of General Education, College & Research Libraries, portal, Journal of Academic Librarianship, Research Strategies, College Teaching, The Teaching Professor*, and *Education*. She was the Chair of the Association of College & Research Libraries' Instruction Section during the 2002–2003 year.

Lijuan Xu (xul@lafayette.edu) is the Library Instruction Coordinator at Lafayette College in Easton, PA. Prior to her work at Lafayette, she was a User Education/Reference Librarian at the University at Albany, SUNY, where she taught four sections of UNL 205, the one-credit Information Literacy course, each semester, and participated in the general library instruction program. Her research interests are in the areas of information literacy and reference. In 1999, she was awarded a scholarship to attend the Association of College and Research Libraries' first Information Literacy immersion program. In 2002, her coauthored article "Motivating Students in Credit-based Information Literacy Courses: Theories and Practice," which appeared in *portal: Libraries and the Academy*, was selected by ALA's Library Instruction Round Table (LIRT) as one of the twenty best instruction articles of the year. She holds an MLS from Clarion University of Pennsylvania and a BA in Library Science from Wuhan University, China.

143